The worship of almighty God is our supreme calling in this life and our eternal destiny in the next. This book by Mike Milton will help all who earnestly desire to glorify and enjoy God in corporate worship and to encourage church leaders to go forward in faith through his miraculous means to achieve his glorious vision.

—**James Bachmann,** senior past
rian Church, Nashville, TN

As a seasoned pastor, Dr. Milton pr
how local congregations can practice what it means to be "Reformed and always reforming." The topics and questions raised in this book are of the sort that will extend the book's usefulness decades after purchase. It is a strong model of the type of spiritual discernment that will not only revitalize congregations but also ignite new fires for churches to pursue their calling in mission of God. Dr. Milton delivers a book that will be useful for not only staff and church officers, but also Sunday school and small group settings.

—**Anthony B. Bradley,** associate professor of theology and ethics, The King's College; editor of *Aliens in the Promised Land*

This challenging book must be read by all Christians. Subjects include God's glory, God's Word, the gospel, church growth, biblical preaching, and prayer—and there is much more to help and encourage churches. Read and pray over its contents!

—**Eryl Davies,** author/research supervisor, Wales Evangelical School of Theology

Mike Milton's book is a gift to the church. Proved in the laboratory of Mike's own pastoral ministry, it exhibits that marvelous mixture of Scripture and story, theology and wise application, objective truth and personal insight, that we have come to expect from one of the foremost leaders and theological educators of our day.

—**R. J. Gore,** professor of systematic theology, Erskine Theological Seminary

Michael Milton is a pastor, a pedagogue, a preacher, a presbyter, a president, and a picker (of guitars, that is). He weaves all these roles into this fine, small work that will be used and used again because of its simplicity, clarity, harmony, and beauty. Don't let its brevity fool you: in a day of Styrofoam castoffs, this is one that you'll read and reread. Its most important value is how it embraces and follows God's revealed mind on ministry, outreach, worship, and preaching.

—**David W. Hall,** senior pastor, Midway Presbyterian Church, Powder Springs, Georgia

Michael Milton is a born leader with a keen mind that cuts to the chase and a heart that burns with passion for the gospel. He comes at this subject as one who has walked the walk. If you are a pastor or worship leader you need to read this book. If you are not a pastor or worship leader, you need to buy two copies, one for yourself and one to give to your pastor. I do not doubt that you and your church will be far better off for reading what Mike Milton has to say in these pages. As a teacher of worship and preaching, I intend to make it required reading for all my students.

—**Robert Leslie Holmes,** Adjunct Professor of Practical Theology, Erskine Theological Seminary

This series of sermons by Mike Milton serves as a helpful and practical guide for churches seeking to minister according to the teaching of the Scriptures. Dr. Milton's focus on the ordinary means of grace is a refreshing alternative to the various "market-driven" methods and trends that continue to influence the church, particularly in North America.

—**Jeffrey K. Jue,** vice president for academic affairs, academic dean, Westminster Theological Seminary

In *Finding a Vision for Your Church*, Mike Milton has provided an excellent resource for those who would lead Christ's church to the glory of God. While intended for pastors and teaching elders, the book provides outstanding guidelines for all those in local church leadership. Beginning his study with "A Burden for God's Glory" and ending with "The Ministry of Prayer," Dr. Milton keeps the focus just where it should be—on him whose church it is. The frequency with which Dr. Milton uses phrases like "hunger for God to be glorified" and "longing for revival and reformation" reminds me of Jonathan Edwards. And the inclusion of questions for reflection at the end of each chapter makes this an excellent resource for practical implementation of the vision presented. I heartily commend this book to all who desire to see Christ's church be all that she can and should be.

—**Samuel Logan,** international director, The World Reformed Fellowship

Assembly Required is a great subtitle at a time when some believers are so turned off by showtime mega-churches that they fall into lone-wolf legalism. Mike Milton eloquently shows us the importance of assembling for worship, prayer, and teaching about grace and compassion.

—**Marvin Olasky,** editor-in-chief, *WORLD* magazine

The resurrection of Christ was such a great experience for the apostle Thomas that when he encountered the risen Lord, all he could say was "My Lord and my God" to Jesus. He worshipped him. When Christ appeared to the disciples in Galilee, Matthew says, "They worshipped him and some doubted." The early church had this fresh experience of resurrection and they "broke bread together and worshipped him." This is what Mike will bring to you and your congregation through his book: the fresh experience of Jesus the Lord. Jesus is exalted through our worship.

—**Henry Luke Orombi,** archbishop, Church of the Province of Uganda

I personally enjoy the privilege of ministry in partnership with RTS and Mike Milton for the cause of biblically healthy and effective churches, and . . . we are once again indebted to God's grace overflowing to us through Mike's endeavor.

—**Harry L. Reeder III,** senior pastor, Briarwood Presbyterian Church

Mike Milton's *Finding a Vision for Your Church* could be yet another "This is how to bring revival to your church" book. Thankfully it is not. Instead, reflecting on Scripture and using his own experience, he introduces us to questions that every church should ask and reflect upon. As a Scotsman, I particularly warmed to the fact that this book is, in my view, applicable outside the North American context as well as within. The vision is God's; by his grace I pray that Mike's book would help us find and implement that wonderful plan the Lord has for his church.

—**David Robertson,** minister, St. Peter's Free Church, Dundee, Scotland

FINDING a VISION for YOUR CHURCH: ASSEMBLY REQUIRED

FINDING a VISION for YOUR CHURCH: ASSEMBLY REQUIRED

MICHAEL A. MILTON

P U B L I S H I N G

P.O. BOX 817 • PHILLIPSBURG • NEW JERSEY 08865-0817

© 2012 Michael A. Milton

All rights reserved. No part of this book may be reproduced, stored in a retrieval system, or transmitted in any form or by any means—electronic, mechanical, photocopy, recording, or otherwise—except for brief quotations for the purpose of review or comment, without the prior permission of the publisher, P&R Publishing Company, P.O. Box 817, Phillipsburg, New Jersey 08865–0817.

Unless otherwise indicated, Scripture quotations are from The Holy Bible, New King James Version. Copyright © 1979, 1980, 1982, Thomas Nelson, Inc.

Scripture quotations marked (NIV) are from the HOLY BIBLE, NEW INTERNATIONAL VERSION®. NIV®. Copyright © 1973, 1978, 1984 by International Bible Society. Used by permission of Zondervan Publishing House. All rights reserved.

Scripture quotations marked (ESV) are from *ESV Bible* ® (*The Holy Bible, English Standard Version* ®). Copyright © 2001 by Crossway Bibles, a publishing ministry of Good News Publishers. Used by permission. All rights reserved.

Scripture quotations marked (NRSV) are from New Revised Standard Version Bible, copyright © 1989 National Council of the Churches of Christ in the United States of America. Used by permission. All rights reserved.

Italics within Scripture quotations indicate emphasis added.

ISBN: 978-1-59638-438-5 (pbk)
ISBN: 978-1-59638-575-7 (ePub)
ISBN: 978-1-59638-576-4 (Mobi)

Printed in the United States of America

Library of Congress Cataloging-in-Publication Data

Milton, Michael A. (Michael Anthony), 1958-
  Finding a vision for your church : assembly required / Michael A. Milton.
-- 1st edition.
     pages cm
  Includes bibliographical references.
  ISBN 978-1-59638-438-5 (pbk.)
  1. Church renewal. 2. Christian life. I. Title.
  BV600.3.M565 2012
  262.001'7--dc23
                              2012035152

This book is dedicated with deep appreciation
and admiration
to the tireless and dedicated gospel service of
my colleagues in ministry:

Scott Brown, the Reverend Ron Brown, the Reverend
Steve Wallace, and the Reverend Rankin Wilbourne;

And to the session and deacons and members of First
Presbyterian Church, Chattanooga, Tennessee;

And to my wife, Mae, who has shown me the reality
of God's love;

And to all our children and grandchildren, with deep,
fatherly love from Dad and Poppy

Contents

Firsthand Testimonials   9

Acknowledgments   13

Introduction   15

1. Let God Come Down!   19
   A Burden for God's Glory

2. Value the Bible   31
   A Passion for God's Word

3. Value the Great Commission   43
   A Heart for God's World

4. Value the Heart of the Gospel   55
   A Commitment to God's Grace

5. Seeing Souls Safe in the Arms of Jesus   69
   A Vision That Is out of This World

6. Seeing Christ Triumphant in Our Generation   79
   A Confident Vision for a Great Harvest

7. Transforming Vision   91
   An Optimistic Ministry

8. Gathering   103
   His Last Words, Our First Work

9. Growing   115
   What Is a Strong Disciple of Jesus Christ?

Contents

10. Sending   127
    Called to Be Taught—Taught to Be Sent

11. Expository Preaching   143
    The Marks of Biblical Preaching

12. Living Worship   157
    Longing for the Courts of the Lord

13. Loving Fellowship   171
    The Church Must Be a Place to Belong

14. Compassionate Outreach   181
    *Becoming the Hands and the Heart of God for a World
    in Need*

15. The Ministry of Prayer   193
    It's All We Have, But It's All We Need

Appendix A: The Implementation of a Vision and
Ministry Plan for a Local Church   209

Appendix B: The Vision and Ministry Statement   215

Notes   231

Resources for Further Study   241

Firsthand Testimonials

Insight from the Pastoral Team Who First Helped Bring the Author's Vision to Pass

VISION DOES NOT happen in a vacuum.

This book, which contains messages that were preached in the early years of our transition into the ministry at First Presbyterian Church of Chattanooga, causes my heart to be deeply moved by my remembrance of colleagues in the gospel ministry, both pastoral and lay. This "band of brothers" went through the process with me. In fact, I hired all of the pastors to help with this vision plan (one minister, the Reverend Ken Camp, who is now with the Lord, was already there as a part-time pastoral care minister). The messages that formed the vision for the ministry of the church have been updated and, hopefully, shaped into such a way that they may be of help to other church planters, church revitalizers, pastors, boards, congregations, and ministry leaders of all sorts. Yet I would be remiss if I did not underscore that ministry cannot happen by merely laying out sermons or vision plans or charts or goals. Vision needs flesh. It must happen cooperatively and collegially with others, who must come alongside and help to shape the vision, inform the vision, challenge the vision, and ultimately "land the vision," as my friend Harry Reeder puts it.

As we complete the manuscript, I cannot help but think about the now seemingly momentous days surrounding the writing of the sermons. We lived them together. It would be the highest form of personal neglect if I failed to mention my esteemed pastoral colleagues in this book.

I am currently reading Winston Churchill's *Great Contemporaries*, and as I write this little endorsement of the pastors and elders and other church leaders who helped me, I am reflecting on the particular passage in the great prime minister's remembrances of Field Marshall Sir Douglas Haig, in which the old Lion said, "But he endured it all; and with such impassivity and matter-of-fact day-to-day routine that I who saw him on [many] occasions—some of them potentially fatal—doubted whether he was not insensitive and indurated to the torment and drama in the shadow of which he dwelt."[1]

Below are some comments from the pastors and church leaders who walked with me through those early days of pastoral transition into years that would bring about realization of much of that vision (though I believe the full fruit will be realized in future days when the potential of ungodly pride will be passed). Indeed, one could very easily make the case that the easiest job was his who preached the principles of our mission, and the truly harder job was the day-to-day landing of that vision which fell upon their shoulders. They performed their duties to Christ so well. It is for that reason that I have dedicated this book, in part, to them.

"These aren't just chapters in a book or words from a distant teacher. Having the privilege of working under and being mentored by Mike Milton, I saw these values lived out, fleshed out, in the local church context. Mike Milton is a pastoral theologian, a pastor's theologian, and these chapters are sure to aid renewal in the local church. Practical. Clear. Biblical."

> —**Rankin Wilbourne,** Minister of Outreach and Missions at First Presbyterian Church during Dr. Milton's pastorate; now Senior Minister of Pacific Crossroads Church in Los Angeles

"When reading books of a practical nature, especially concerning the pastoral ministry, one intuitively knows if the work is born out of experience and will be worthwhile. I can assure you that you will sense immediately that this book is born out of practical experience because I was there, watching, learning, and participating as one of the pastoral staff alongside Mike Milton while he was the senior pastor at First Presbyterian Church in Chattanooga, Tennessee. I don't believe I am exaggerating to say that if you pricked Mike anywhere, he would bleed pastoral wisdom. As you read, I believe your heart will be moved and motivated by the biblical instruction and love for Christ's flock exhibited in this book."

> —**M. Steve Wallace,** Chief of Staff and Executive Minister at First Presbyterian Church during Dr. Milton's pastorate; now Chief of Staff and Chief Operating Officer at Reformed Theological Seminary

"Dr. Milton first wrote these messages to cast a vision for his own assembly, and this collection, along with the accompanying practical appendices, is founded on the Word of God and rich with Scripture. He has thoroughly punctuated his own insight with historical illustrations, everyday examples, and the words of other scholar-preachers. From his own scholarship and experiences he answers the question, 'What does a true biblical church look like?', presenting with clarity the elements of a truly sacred assembly of believers in a Spirit-filled church. A great blessing for pastors and laity alike."

—**Scott N. Brown Jr.,** Clerk of Session at First Presbyterian Church, both now and during Dr. Milton's pastorate

"The heartbeat of this book is Mike Milton's love for those foundational, ordinary means that lead to extraordinary works of God in ministry. My recommendation: read *Finding a Vision for Your Church: Assembly Required* once and then pick it up annually as a helpful yardstick and corrective to gauge where your ministry is on track and where you've veered off course. As I read it I am reminded of Mike's patient mentorship of me and am thankful for the opportunity to experience it afresh in print."

—**Ron Brown,** Minister of Discipleship at First Presbyterian Church during Dr. Milton's pastorate; now Reformed University Fellowship campus minister at Covenant College in Lookout Mountain, Georgia

Acknowledgments

THE LORD HAS BROUGHT so many blessings to me. As I write these acknowledgments, I'm coming out of a season of sickness. During that time, I "enjoyed" a refreshing time of reacquaintance with my God. It was as if, as I've said in a recent sermon, I was allowed "to rest in God before running in ministry." There was another reacquaintance, however, and that was with my wife, Mae. I will never forget her faithfulness as she sought to nurse me back to health in the presence of a most mysterious illness (which the Almighty mercifully healed). I came to understand the meaning of the vow, "in sickness and in health," in a more meaningful way. Thus, in the summer of 2011, as I prepare this manuscript, I acknowledge the merciful hand of almighty God and the extension of his hand in the hand of my wife, Mae. I have been greatly blessed by God. I have been greatly encouraged and supported by my wife.

I also want to express my gratitude to the Rev. Marvin Padgett of P&R Publishing Company. Stitching together sermons into meaningful chapters that have direction, a singular focus, and intentionality concerning a particular readership, is no small assignment. Marvin helped me grasp that reality. Writing this book was, therefore, more than submitting previously written sermons for publication. I spent many hours back in the Word of God, writing and rewriting, clarifying and sharpening, in response to Marvin's challenge. In the end, I leave the results to the reader. I take full responsibility for anything lacking herein, but give thanks to Marvin for help-ing me to strengthen this work. However it may be received, I assure you that it is better than the first manuscript he received! Thank you, Marvin.

I am indebted to Amanda Martin at P&R for her insightful reading of the work and application of her solid Grove City College training to the study section. It is my prayer that the fruit of her work will be seen in believers and entire congre-gations who settle for nothing less than a biblical vision and the blessings that follow. I also want to thank Ian Thompson for his wise counsel in helping to discover the best title and subtitle to describe the book. And I am always appreciative of the excellent editing by Aaron Gottier. P&R remains a favorite publisher of mine because of one reason: outstanding people.

I also want to thank the executive committee of Reformed Theological Seminary, as well as my colleagues at the seminary, especially Dr. Ric Cannada, Rev. Lyn Perez, Ms. Wendy Sim-mons, and Rev. Steve Wallace. Quite simply, this work could not have been completed without their support. Thank you.

And now I pray that the Spirit of the living God, who breathed forth the words that I have sought to exposit in these pages, will perfect my praise and gratitude to the triune God, to whom this and all of my life is dedicated.

Introduction

FINDING A VISION for Your Church: Assembly Required began as a series of messages that I preached at First Presbyterian Church of Chattanooga, Tennessee. I was called to that historic congregation as their senior pastor in December 2000. My first sermon there delivered on the first Sunday in February 2001. After giving my testimony from Philippians 1:1–6, I began to preach a series of messages from selected portions of God's Word that would help our congregation focus on our common life together as the church. I desired something more than just an opening series that might get us all acquainted. I was praying for a filling of the Holy Spirit for me and for the congregation. I was asking God that he might reveal himself to us in a fresh way. I was praying for revival. Many others were praying to that supernatural end as well.

We did in fact see the hand of the Lord move at that time. Let there be no overstatement of the facts. There was no visible, demonstrable, citywide movement from on high, as far as I could perceive it (and I have been blessed to see such genuine revival—in Albania, days after "the wall" fell in that Balkan country, releasing the poor people from the tyranny of Communism and ushering in a movement of God that created a hunger for him; once seeing it, one can never forget it, and once experiencing it, one can never get over it). There was, however, a new spark of life in my own heart in those days. As pastor, I was also allowed to observe the movement of the Holy Spirit in individual lives in our congregation and also in our community.

One of the greatest challenges I felt that I had then, and continue to have now, as one who has been elected to serve one of the great theological seminaries in our nation, is to believe and preach with conviction that the church is more than we see here today. The church is a sacred assembly, called out by almighty God, saved from the auction block of sin and shame and hell, and redeemed to fulfill God's purposes in the world today. She is also called by God to become his everlasting people in a new heaven and a new earth. How we get from where we are today to that place in eternity future is a story of its own. And that is what this book is about.

This book, then, is not just a definition *of* the church; it is a declaration *about* the church. The church is, in fact, the very body of the Lord Jesus Christ, existing by the power of his Word, his life, his atoning death, his resurrection, his ascension, and his reign, and living in anticipation of his glorious return. It is my conviction that this declaration, using the very means of grace that God has left his church—Word, sacrament, and prayer—has an evangelistic power embedded within it. Therefore, to proclaim the reality of the church, whether from the pulpit as a preacher, or in the seminary classroom as a professor, or on the assembly line as a worker, or in the Army motor pool as a private, is to engage the world with the gospel of Jesus Christ.

As I write this introduction, I pray to the Lord Jesus Christ that these messages will be of blessing to you. I pray that since I delivered them in those first days of transition at a new charge and again in seminary settings, and now as I have edited this book to reach a broader readership, the Holy Spirit will convey the enduring truths of his Word to each and every reader. I pray that pastors, elders, deacons, and church leaders of all sorts, with all of the people who worship with them, week in and week out, will come to see the glory and power that is resident in the church—a power that, when unleashed, can transform lives and bring healing to our wounded world. Thus, I would lay a cornerstone for this book with the words of the apostle Paul when he wrote about the church in his epistle to the Ephesians. In their world of confusion and bewilderment, the people of God did not fully comprehend the power of Christ at work within them. They, like we today, needed a fresh vision of the church—of the truth of Christ in his church—that would bring about a God-wrought vision for what he would do through them—a vision for personal, corporate, and global transformation. By God's grace, the early church received that blessing. May we receive it now. It is simply this ascription of praise:

> Now to him who is able to do far more abundantly than all that we ask or think, according to the power at work within us, to him be glory in the church and in Christ Jesus throughout all generations, forever and ever. Amen. (Eph. 3:20–21 esv)

1

Let God Come Down!

A Burden for God's Glory

ISAIAH 64

This is revival, dear people! This is a sovereign act of God! This is the moving of God's Spirit, I believe in answer to the prevailing prayer of men and women who believed that God was a Covenant-keeping God, and must be true to His Covenant engagement. —*Duncan Campbell*[1]

We say our prayers, but have we ever prayed? Do we know anything about this encounter, this meeting? Have we the assurance of sins forgiven? Are we free from ourselves and self-concern, that we may intercede? Have we a real burden for the glory of God, and the name of the Church? Have we this concern for those who are outside? And are we pleading with God for his own name's sake, because of his own promises, to hear us and to answer us? Oh, my God, make of us intercessors. —*David Martyn Lloyd-Jones*[2]

IN ISAIAH 64, Isaiah had seen the very courts of heaven. But his job was to preach to a very earth-bound people. Isaiah had a burden. His burden wasn't just for Israel. His burden was for the glory of God:

> Oh, that You would rend the heavens!
> That You would come down!
> That the mountains might shake at Your presence—
> As fire burns brushwood,
> As fire causes water to boil—
> To make Your name known to Your adversaries,
> That the nations may tremble at Your presence! (Isa. 64:1–2)

Casting a Vision

When a new minister takes up his sacred post, many in the congregation may wonder about his vision for the church. Will he build upon the past or move in new directions?

Vision is a word that is not only overused but also misunderstood. In today's culture, *vision* implies carefully crafted statements, ranging from the simple to the sophisticated, for just about any corporation or organization. Everything from a Fortune 500 company to a small, family-run business has its own vision statement. And there is much to be commended in having one. However, a vision statement alone doesn't ensure success. In recent American corporate history, Enron Corporation had a laudable vision statement—before it became the biggest bankruptcy in U.S. history.

Of course, a vision statement for a church is vastly different from a vision statement for a corporation. The church's vision statement, its very identity and purpose, must be thoroughly grounded in the Word of God. Nothing else will do.

A church can have a finely crafted vision, but be completely out of the will of the Lord, unbiblical, and lacking in the power of the Holy Spirit who attends his Word. A church can be an ecclesiastical Enron, all puffed up with religious smoke and mirrors, but having nothing of eternal value—or, as Paul put it, "having a form of godliness but denying its power" (2 Tim. 3:5).

The overriding purpose of this book is to cast a vision for the church, for God's holy bride. That vision must be weighed on the scales of Scripture. Or, to put it another way, the church's vision must stand with the Bible: "To the law and to the testimony!" (Isa. 8:20).

Before going one step further, there are three caveats. First, when casting a new vision for a church, you must recognize that there are powerful forces of good already in place in the church where you are placed. Dreams dreamed long ago and visions cast before you were born are still at work today. Second, recognize that it takes time to formulate a vision. Be patient. Ministers and lay leaders should spend the early months of their ministry listening to what God has been doing and is doing in their midst. Third, this book is not just for ministers and lay leaders. This book about the church is for all of us who are believers in Christ, who are members of that holy bride that Christ is perfecting. Now, more than ever, we need to think biblically about the church. She is under attack from without, and often, unwittingly, from within.

I have found that, as a minister serving as a seminary leader, I am often called upon to enter into discussions with believers about various challenges facing congregations. In most cases, the problem has something to do with the nature of the church in our day. It may involve a lack of understanding of role relationships in the church, or the express signs of a true church, or the scripturally revealed purpose of the church, or the biblically disclosed methods for the church to realize her glorious goals in the world. It may just be that we fail to understand the eschatological vision of the church—that we are not where we are going, but we are on our way by God's grace.

The Burden: A Holy Dissatisfaction

When the Word of God is read in its entirety, you come to understand that it begins with a burden. That burden, simply stated, is God's burden for his own creation. Man was unable to keep God's law and fell away from his Creator. This grieved God. According to Ephesians 1, God saw this before the foundation of the world and took steps to remedy the problem. After the fall, the rest of Scripture is a record of God working out his covenant of grace; that is, God, by grace, has been doing for man what man could not do for himself. It is a record of God ordaining that he would come down to fulfill the requirements of his law and to pour out his wrath for sin upon himself as a propitiation for the sins of man. God was burdened for his own creation.

So the vision of the Bible begins with a burden. Therefore, any outline for a church's vision must begin with a burden. When believers come to understand that burden, when they develop a heart and a passion for something that grieves them, that pains them, that creates desire, then vision emerges. A biblical vision is a divine solution that lifts the burden.

Turning to Isaiah 64, you see that Isaiah was a man with a burden for God's glory in his own generation. You begin to understand what that burden entailed when you read the prophet's plaintive words, "Oh, that."

Job uses this phrase more than anyone in Scripture. He cries out from the depth of his soul, "Oh, that my words were written! Oh, that they were inscribed in a book!" (Job 19:23).

David uses the same opening in his exasperation over the sin of the wicked: "Oh, that men would give thanks to the LORD for His goodness, and for His wonderful works to the children of men!" (Ps. 107:21). And Isaiah the prophet cries out, "Oh, that You would . . . come down!" (Isa. 64:1).

"Oh, that" expresses a holy dissatisfaction with the way things are in comparison with who God is. The prophet has seen God, experienced his glory, known his salvation, desired that Israel would know him, and so was dissatisfied.

There is evidence throughout the Bible that Christians are to be dissatisfied. Christians are enjoined to be content—but that refers to our circumstances, not to God's glory!

Moses had a burden. When he first had a burden for his Hebrew brethren, he took matters into his own hands and ended up herding goats in the back forty of Midian. But then God manifested himself in a burning bush, and when Moses took his rod and marched into Pharaoh's court, that man had a burden for God's glory.

Paul knew God's glory in grace and could never be content with ordinary religion. He would sacrifice all, count every gain as rubbish, put himself at risk, and take on any earthly power. For what? That he might know Christ and the power of his resurrection. Paul was a burdened man. He was burdened for God's glory. He had experienced Christ and thought that the world would be unworthy until every knee would bow and every tongue would confess that Jesus is Lord to the glory of the Father.

Thus, every vision begins with a burden, a holy dissatisfaction. "Oh, that" is the cry of a person or a church that has known the grace of God, has come to know the joy of a life surrendered to the compassionate Christ, and is discontent until God is glorified and worshipped and enjoyed.

The church today must have a burden. We must stand like Isaiah and say, "Oh, that God would come down in our community. There are people who need Christ. Oh, that God would come down to our nation. Oh, that God would come down to the Muslim people, to the African people, to Hispanics in Los Angeles, to smug, comfortable, pretend Christians who are not living to give God the glory."

The church must be burdened—burdened for the glory of God.

Isaiah's "oh, that" reveals his holy discontent, but the unfolding passage reveals more.

The Relief: Genuine Revival

The person who has experienced the living God is burdened for his glory in revival. Isaiah writes, "Oh, that You would rend the heavens! That You would come down!" (Isa. 64:1). Isaiah is dissatisfied. He is burdened, and the relief that he seeks is genuine revival.

When Isaiah writes, "Oh, that You would . . . come down," do you think he is just interested in springtime revival meetings by a visiting clergyman? Nothing could be further from his mind! The prophet is burdened by a lackadaisical religion. Isaiah doesn't want religion. He wants God! In this passage, we see mountains trembling, fires setting the forest ablaze, water boiling. It is a veritable eruption of divine presence on earth that this man of God yearns for.

This, beloved, is what you must pray for. Pray for revival in this generation—a genuine movement of God in which he is honored and glorified in this hour of world history.

Paul Johnson, in his book *History of the American People*, notes that American history is a history of revival. As you look upon our nation—our desperate need, and our evangelical churches going from one faddish program to another, just to grow membership roles—we must cry out, "Oh, that God would come down!" We need genuine revival, a moment of God that transcends our natural abilities and makes everyone know that he has come down.

The church today must have a burden for revival in our time.

The Result: Reformation

Note further that Isaiah longs for even more. He reveals the focus of his burden for revival: "Make your name known to your enemies and cause the nations to quake before you!" (Isa. 64:2 NIV). Isaiah is burdened for reformation as well as revival. The person who has experienced the living God is also burdened for reformation.

Reformation, in the biblical sense, is the transformation of society as the result of the transformation of the human soul because of God's own work. It is the burden of a child of God who has come to know the glory of God's holiness. The child of God, like the prophet, is offended that men continue to sin in the face of this holy God. Christians are people, like the prophets of old, who are filled with righteous indignation because God is not worshipped and honored properly. First you have a burden for the glory of God, then for revival, and then for reformation in our day.

As a child, you must have encountered bullies. Sandy was such a bully. He was known principally for his almost uncanny command of an ever-growing volume of curse words. No child ever had a more filthy mouth. But other kids began to pray for Sandy, and one child invited him to church. There was a new preacher at the church, and that was an excuse for Sandy to go. Over time, Sandy was saved, and he changed—radically. He eventually led his entire family to Christ, felt the call to ministry, and today is a widely known Baptist preacher. The point is, reformation came to Sandy's house, and as his heart was changed, his speech and behavior were changed.

You must have a burden for God's glory in our world today. Are you tired of vulgarity on the airwaves of our nation, horrified by abortions being given legal protection, struck with righteous indignation over our great Christian churches ordaining unrepentant sinners to the pulpit, and offended by the sexualizing of everything and the open attack by Madison Avenue on our children's innocence? If so, you have a burden for God's glory in the land.

The church must be burdened by the ugliness of sin in our generation and by the bondage, pain, and brokenness that accompany it. The church must long for the reformation of our land and pray that God would come down and do something in the hearts of our countrymen, that God would supernaturally renew the minds of the people in our family and our community.

The Method: Salvation

But the question comes then, How can we be saved? Indeed, this is Isaiah's question in Isaiah 64:5:

How then can we be saved? (NIV)
And we need to be saved. (NKJV)

The answer is found in Isaiah 64:8:

But now, O LORD,
You are our Father.

Why can you expect an answer to the prayer, "God, come down"? There are two reasons.

Because of the fatherhood of God. "Oh, God, come down!" That statement is our hope. You must fix your eyes on the very nature of God as he reveals himself to us. He is our Father. The fatherhood of God assures us that he will answer our prayers.

God as Father desires the salvation of his children, our healing, and the transformation of this world more than any pastor could. This is the testimony of Scripture:

While we were still sinners, Christ died for us. (Rom. 5:8)

God was in Christ reconciling the world to Himself, not imputing their trespasses to them. (2 Cor. 5:19)

For God so loved the world that He gave His only begotten Son. (John 3:16)

Benjamin B. Warfield of old Princeton Seminary taught that the emphasis of John 3:16 is on the love of God in comparison to the wickedness of the world. He "so loved the world." God's love is greater than our sin. His grace and mercy are greater than our little rebellion.

When a pastor is burdened for God's glory in revival and reformation, he wants what God wants. And those prayers are bound to be answered, for God's own nature, his fatherhood, assures us that he will come down.

Jesus assures us of this truth when he says, "All that the Father gives Me will come to Me, and the one who comes to Me I will by no means cast out" (John 6:37).

Because of the work of the Son. The other answer is in Isaiah 64:9: "Do not remember our sins forever" (NIV).

He didn't. God, before the foundation of the world, made a sacred pledge to himself, a covenant of grace, that he would assume the sins of his people himself. Thus, on Calvary's cross, the central act of cosmic history took place. Paul wrote, "God made him who had no sin to be sin for us, so that in him we might become the righteousness of God" (2 Cor. 5:21 NIV).

Your burdens were lifted at Calvary. And therein lies your hope, your answer, and the vision of your life, your church, and your family. The love of God in Jesus Christ gives you optimism in your day. God will be successful. You may begin the work of prayer, of preaching, and of witness in our day. You may not see the salvation en masse that you long to see, but God's kingdom will be successful. He will bring all of his people in. This gives you unbounded confidence in your work in the church. Believers stand on the winning side.

Conclusion

Isaiah 64 draws a surprising beginning. It teaches that developing a vision begins by confessing a holy dissatisfaction with the way things are and hungering for God to be glorified. You must admit your longing for revival and reformation, and recognize that the answer to that longing is found at the foot of the cross.

A story will illustrate this point. A minister once preached a message on the soul's desire for God. After the service, an elder came to the minister and said, "I go to church. I pray. I do everything a good Christian is supposed to do. But when you talk about desiring God, I'm lost. When you talk about panting for the presence of God, I have no idea what you are talking about. I know the catechism, but I don't know about this passion for Christ or this love for him. Can you tell me what's missing?" What that man was missing was a true awareness of God's glory, of his own sinfulness, and of God's love and grace in Jesus Christ at Calvary's cross. Over time, he came to know God's love and grace. For to know him is to love him and desire him. To desire him is to long for him, to be burdened for his crown rights as King of kings and Lord of lords in our generation.

Isaiah was burdened for the glory of God because he had experienced God's glory in his own life. Similarly, if the church doesn't know God's grace, if its leaders don't experience the glory of God in prayer, if families don't know his mercy and his peace through seeking him in prayer and worship in their own homes, then the church will have no burden.

Before you can cast a vision for your church, you must come to know your sin, your need, and his holiness. You must also know his love in sending his own Son to die for your sinful condition. When you know him in that way and you look out on a world of brokenness and sin and shame—across the ocean, across the nation, across the city, and, yes, across your own living room—then your soul will be burdened to cry with Isaiah, "Oh, that God would come down!"

Questions for Reflection

1. Reflect on your church's vision, even if you have no official statement of it. What do the leaders and congregation expect from the church? Are their expectations grounded in the Word of God? Are their expectations in alignment?

How can the church encourage unity and holiness of vision?

2. Do the visions of past leaders play a role in your church's decision making? If they do, evaluate them. Are they hindering the church's true mission, or do they help to focus and unite the church? How might those in leadership communicate their vision and their predecessors' vision to the congregation?

3. Consider how you can pray for vision and revival. What burdens might your church be called to lift? What are the concerns and passions of the congregation? How could your church's location come into play?

4. Write the rough outline of a vision statement for your church or revise the current one. How can you personally contribute to this vision?

5. Examine your heart. What motivates your desire for revival? How must the gospel change you?

Prayer

Oh, that my heart would be burdened for your glory in this generation; *oh, that* you would send your Spirit to renew and revive me and your church to take the gospel of the cross to this generation!

2

Value the Bible

A Passion for God's Word

REVELATION 2:1–4; 2 TIMOTHY 3

The Lord does not shine upon us, except when we take his Word as our light. —*John Calvin*[1]

THE CHURCH AT EPHESUS had left its first love (Rev. 2:1–4). Commentators wonder about the full meaning of this, but the Bible is saying that this church, founded by Paul and pastored by Timothy, simply left the things they loved at first.

These "first things" may be clearly discerned from Scripture and will help you stay on course as a faithful minister of God's Word shepherding your congregation. As you begin to develop your church's vision, you must keep in mind three important guiding principles. The first of these three, having a passion for God's Word, will be considered in this chapter.

An Internal Guidance System

You can lose your way without the right internal guidance system.

News of a dolphin that mysteriously made its way out of the Atlantic Ocean and into a canal in New York State made national headlines. Trapped in the canal and away from the natural habitat of the expansive deep, the creature died and washed ashore. A team of marine biologists and other scientists was called in to examine the remains of the poor animal and solve the mystery of why it came inland. The autopsy revealed that a parasite had attached itself to the part of the dolphin's brain that served as an internal guidance system. The dolphin had become internally confused, had lost its way, and had died.

Have you ever witnessed a church that once swam deep in God's grace, but somewhere along the way had lost its way? What happened? It doesn't take much of an autopsy to answer the question. A parasite of sorts had attached itself to the internal guidance system of that church, and they didn't know which way to go. The church was washed up, was gasping for breath, and was about to die.

Many pastors can tell stories about Christians who talk about life in the open sea of God's goodness, about better times when they swam with joy, when they dreamed dreams and frolicked in the streams of life as children of God. But somehow they went astray. They ended up in a foreign place, in a place they never wanted to be. They didn't know how they got there. They felt confused and lost, and as far as they could tell, they were beached and dying.

You know people like that, don't you? And you know of churches like that, as well.

It's no use talking about a vision for the church today—your local church and mine—unless we all address the internal guidance system for that vision. A godly vision must be guided by divine precepts. Jesus called these "your first love." These are the first things of ministry, the core values of ministry. If your ministry and your Christian life aren't guided by these things, the greatest vision could become your worst nightmare.

Paul founded the church at Ephesus, and Timothy pastored it. Yet, despite that great heritage of faith, the church at Ephesus left her first love and was on the verge of being washed up. What did she leave behind? How did she get off course? What was her first love? Whatever else this might have involved, it most certainly included a love—a passion—for God's Word.

Here you clearly see what God has provided for every believer and every church. Here you locate the divine guidance system as you begin a new pastorate. Here you find your heavenly compass, your operating system, your lifeline to God's will. As you launch out into the deep waters of ministry, as you forge a vision for your ministry, you must have a passion for God's Word.

Recognize, however, that having a passion for God's Word is more than just acknowledging belief in the Bible. We are talking about a realization that without God's Word in your life and in the lives of your congregation, giving you vision and renewing your mind, you will be lost. It is the fundamental commitment of one who, like King David, knows the joy of following God's Word and the heartache of ignoring it, and who therefore cries out, "With my whole heart I have sought You; oh, let me not wander from Your commandments!" (Ps. 119:10). As you consider the teaching of 2 Timothy 3, you must have a passion for God's Word. Here are two major reasons why this is so:

God's Word Reveals the Threats That Will Cause You to Wander (2 Tim. 3:1–9).

A favorite prank of teenagers is to take road signs and turn them around so that newcomers will be led astray. This is exactly what happened at Ephesus. There were threats to lead the people away from God, to upset the ministry of Timothy, and in this passage Paul warns them of that.

Second Timothy 3:1 tells us to "know this." The NIV translates it, "But mark this: There will be terrible times in the last days." When Paul uses the phrase "last days," he is not talking about some future time "out there" and of no present use to Timothy. On the contrary, Paul is warning Timothy that these "last days" are upon him! Paul's letters show us that with the resurrection and ascension of Christ, the last days have come. They are here, and they are accompanied, not only by a growth of the kingdom of God, but also by the growth of evil. And there are certain dangers that can cause you to wander:

The threat of moral depravity (2 Tim. 3:1–4). This list of debaucheries portrays a man who places himself at the center of the world to the neglect of his family, his neighbors, his nation, and God. This is a veritable snapshot of the day in which we live, yet the Bible keeps us on track in the midst of an onslaught of evil. If you are to carry forward the work of the Lord, you must steer clear of the moral dangers lurking in every corner. Our nation is awash in moral perversity. What is good is called evil, and what is evil is called good. How do you follow God's vision in such an environment? Only by heeding the Word of God.

The threat of religious depravity (2 Tim. 3:5). Next Paul talks about a form of godliness that lacks the power thereof. Now, as then, there is a mind-set in the church that seeks to have a Christ without a cross, a Savior without a resurrection, a God without power, and, most seriously, a Bible without authority.

Americans measure success by the numbers. Pastors are often guilty of measuring themselves and the success of their ministry by the numbers—most notably, church membership. We have witnessed the rise of megachurches and cannot help but compare them to the small, fledgling congregations. A minister of one of those fast-growing churches once confided his secret to growth: he was no longer entangled by the belief in the inerrancy of Scripture. My dear friend, this man had a church with a form of godliness, but there was no power. If there is no belief in a supernatural Bible, then there is no power to save souls, to restore lives, to build families, or to prepare people to follow God all the way home. A supernatural work requires a supernatural Word. You must hold a vision that relies upon supernatural power that flows, not from form, but from the Word of God.

The threat of a fleshly Christianity (2 Tim. 3:6). Paul speaks about those who "worm their way into homes and gain control over weak-willed women, who are loaded down with sins and are swayed by all kinds of evil desires" (NIV).

This portrays sensual, pagan religious practices. This is a Christian who lacks holiness in his life and is infected with the lusts of this present evil age. You know that wandering away from Christ's righteousness can stop ministry, destroy testimonies, and suspend the work of the gospel. So take heed. Beware of the siren song of this present evil age as you hear the Bible expose it so clearly.

The threat of a false intellectualism (2 Tim. 3:7). Paul describes this as "always learning but never able to acknowledge the truth" (NIV). In other words, there is a danger of accumulating knowledge without the wisdom of God's Word. We hear a great deal about education being the answer to our problems, but we also hear about highly educated families that are being ripped apart by foolish decisions. Education without Christ cannot sustain a happy marriage, raise godly children, offer abundant life, or inherit eternal life. Yet in our day, as in Paul's, this mind-set pervades our culture.

The threat of diabolical activity (2 Tim. 3:8). Finally, in this verse, Paul compares the workers of iniquity in the last days to Jannes and Jambres, the magicians in the court of Pharaoh who opposed Moses and the word of God. In our day, we are witnesses to a growing interest in spirituality apart from God's Word. Go into a bookstore today and you will see shelves lined with volumes on religion and ways to God apart from faith in Jesus Christ. These are imposters and will lead you astray. Our culture is seemingly willing to embrace every form of spirituality except the faith that says: Jesus is the way, the truth, and the life. Be aware of this error, and be clear that there is no way to God except through his own appointed path: repentance and faith in the life, death, and resurrection of Jesus Christ.

In preparation for a road trip, you first research the best route and mark out the dangers you might encounter, including bridges that are out, roads under construction, and rush hour traffic—and this planning helps you to arrive at your destination on time.

This is what the Bible does for you. You cannot move forward into the future unless you are committed to the Word of God, for Scripture alone will show you the dangers that could lead you astray. And what is your goal? To arrive safely home and be welcomed into the arms of your Savior, and not to wander alone in the desert.

In 2 Timothy 3:1–9, the apostle is telling Timothy about the dangers that could cause you to wander. But in 2 Timothy 3:10–17, Paul shows Timothy the truth that will lead you home. You should have a passion for God's Word because:

The Bible Alone Will Help You to Find Your Way Home (2 Tim. 3:10–17).

The Bible helps you to find your way by leading you with real-life examples (2 Tim. 3:10–12). "But you have carefully followed my doctrine, manner of life, purpose, faith, long-suffering, love, perseverance, persecutions, afflictions" (2 Tim. 3:10–11). Here Paul is saying that Timothy might learn how to live by observing him. Likewise, you, too, can learn how to build your life by studying the lives of Paul, David, Peter, Abraham, Moses, Jonah, Sarah, Esther, Hannah, and so many more in Scripture. In his Word, God has given you his truth in human flesh, so that you can relate to it and learn to live a godly life. In other words, the Bible is a guide to help you find your way home through living examples.

Since the Bible helps you to find your way home, you must prioritize the Bible in your own home (2 Tim. 3:14–15). "But you must continue in the things which you have learned . . . knowing from whom you have learned them, and that from childhood you have known the Holy Scriptures" (2 Tim. 3:14–15). Here Paul refers to something he introduced in chapter 1, namely, that Timothy had the benefit of having been taught by his grandmother Lois and his mother Eunice.

You need to renew your passion for God's Word in order to teach it to the little ones. As you launch out in a new ministry, you must emphasize family worship and Bible reading. The testimony of families in your congregation opening the Word of God and reading it before bedtime will bring great strength, not only to other families, but also to your community, to the nation, and ultimately to the next generation. But it does even more: it builds spiritual giants, like Timothy, for the future. Family worship, even ten minutes every day, will forge men and women of God who will be used of the Lord to change the world.

The Bible helps you find your way because it comes from the mind of almighty God (2 Tim. 3:15–17). Paul says that the Word of God will make us wise for salvation. We can make it safely home only if we know the way. The Bible makes us wise for salvation by showing us that there is something to be saved from. We are sinners, under the wrath of God. The Bible shows us that the only way to be saved is through God's own provision in his Son, whose sinless life is imputed to us when by faith we receive him as our Lord. Your sins and mine are then imputed to Christ, who bore them on the cross. This is the wisdom of God, the very mind of God.

In 2 Timothy 3:16–17, Paul sums up his entire argument by saying that the Bible was breathed out by the Lord. This is what is meant when Paul writes, "All Scripture is given by inspiration of God." Everything you need for your future pastorate is given to you in this book. Everything you desire in terms of fulfillment, meaning, hope, and purpose is found within these sacred pages.

You know the familiar children's Bible song:

The B-I-B-L-E,
Yes, that's the book for me.
I stand alone on the Word of God,
The B-I-B-L-E.

That song is just repeating 2 Timothy 3:16–17. It is really saying that the Bible is sufficient. And sufficiency is the real issue.

Before he died, James Montgomery Boice maintained that the question facing the church in the twenty-first century would not be that of the nature of Scripture, but that of the sufficiency of Scripture.[2] Many are trying to achieve their vision through human means. Too many think that we can't grow the church by just teaching the Bible. Too many are deceived into thinking that we can't truly offer a cure for the diseases of the human soul by only teaching the Bible. But this text tells us that the Word of God is sufficient "for doctrine, for reproof, for correction, for instruction in righteousness, that the man of God may be complete, thoroughly equipped for every good work." Your core conviction must be that the Word of God is sufficient to realize the salvation of souls and to edify the people of God to make a happy home and to inherit an eternal home.

If you have wavered or wandered from that conviction, turn to God in prayer and cry out for a faith that rests all your life on this blessed book. This book is the divine revelation of God Almighty, which will (1) keep you from wandering and (2) show you the way home. That is the simple truth of 2 Timothy 3.

As you formulate your vision for the years ahead, you must be motivated by a passion for God's Word.

The Power of a Bloodstained Book

John MacArthur, the noted radio preacher from Grace Community Church in Southern California, has a Bible in his study that is one of the first ever printed in English. But that is not as notable as this next truth. When he secured the

Bible, the previous owner showed him that the pages were stained. MacArthur, being a collector of old Bibles, had seen water stains and coffee stains and the like before. But this stain was different. He took it to an authority and had it verified. The stain on the pages of that Bible was human blood. The Bible was said to have been in the possession of a sixteenth-century Englishman who was persecuted for owning it. That anonymous person from long ago had a passion for God's Word. That man's blood was a testimony to his passion.[3]

It is doubtful whether the proof of our passion for the Bible will ever have to be given in blood. But on the pages of every Bible is blood—the blood of Jesus Christ, shed for the sins of every vile sinner who would ever trust in him. And there is power in that blood. It pleased God to disperse that power through the reading and the preaching of his Word, the Bible. And so, your vision as a church must rest on this bloodstained book. Your life will have to be built upon this book if you are ever to realize God's vision for your life.

Make sure the Word of God is your first love. Make sure you never leave your first love. Make sure that you pause right now to recommit yourself to bringing your life daily to the Word of God and to hiding it in your heart. Then you, too, will experience the power of God in your life as you've never known it before. To know the Christ who shed his blood for you is to come to know a love like no other. And he is first known by experiencing him and his will for your life on every pulsating page of the Bible. For Jesus Christ is not only called the Son of God, but also called the very Word of God. To love Christ, then, is to truly have a passion for God's Word.

✝

Questions for Reflection

1. Think of the ways in which you may have devalued God's Word through compromise or neglect, either publicly or privately. What steps should you take to rectify this?

2. How can your church support its members as they participate in personal devotions and family worship? Consider providing resources, suggestions, or an explanatory class.

3. Do you study the Bible outside church activities, or, if a pastor or teacher, outside your sermon or lesson preparation? Think of the approaches to personal devotions you have found most fruitful in your life (journaling, reading through the Bible in a year, using devotional supplements, etc.). How can you pursue a deeper delight in God's Word without imposing burdens on yourself or others?

4. Does your church as a whole understand the authority of Scripture? How does your church express confidence in the Bible's authority? How might greater understanding of biblical authority be promoted in the congregation?

5. Examine your heart. Do you lack confidence in the authority and inerrancy of God's Word? Pray for comfort, understanding, and guidance. How must the gospel change you?

Prayer

Father, you spoke to us not by images but by your Word. We are often drawn to the unbelieving urges to return to the image, the idea of our own, the imaginations of our hearts, the counsel of our own supposed wisdom, rather than the propositional truth of your Word, the Bible. Help us not only to repent of this tendency, but to search the Scriptures with prayer and to seek you and your Word. We affirm that your Word is bound together by the blood of the covenant in Jesus Christ and we long to come under his lordship. Help us to listen. Help us to hear. Help us to trust. Help us to preach, sing, pray, and study your Word. And as we do, come to us through the same Spirit who wrote that Word. In Jesus' name. Amen.

3

Value the Great Commission

A Heart for God's World

LUKE 15:1–2; 11–32

I think I can say, I have never risen a morning without thinking how I could bring more souls to Christ.
—*Robert Murray M'Cheyne*[1]

CAN A BELIEVER ever have a passion for God's Word without a corresponding passion for God's world? In the setting of one of the most unforgettable parables in the teaching of our Lord, beginning in Luke 15:1–2, you'll find God's answer.

Heart Recall

We live in a day of manufacturers' recalls. But can you imagine a recall of a heart? Several years ago, a company issued a recall for 487 pacemakers, almost all of them in the chests of patients! Apparently those pacemakers had a defect that threatened to disrupt the electric charge to the patient's heart.[2]

The truth is that some Christians may need a heart recall. For numerous reasons, the faulty mechanisms of the old heart—old ways, old sins, bad attitudes, deep-seated resentments, and ugly bitterness—might begin to fire their sinister charges and disrupt the healthy flow of grace and joy. In some cases, saved, sanctified, and otherwise maturing believers become infested with terrible symptoms that, upon close inspection, reveal a faulty heart—a heart that doesn't care about the lost, a heart that is hardened toward those who are without Jesus Christ. In other cases (and these are the worst), the person who seems to be a Christian is not even a Christian at all.

Our Lord was apparently dealing with such hard-hearted listeners in the passage from Luke. Controversy began because "sinners drew near to Him." This disturbed the self-righteous religious leaders of that day. It always does. So Jesus, seeking both to disclose the hard-heartedness of the Pharisees and the scribes and to comfort the humble hearts of repentant sinners, displayed the heart of God. He began telling stories about lost things.

This series of stories is powerful as it moves from the least expensive to the most expensive of lost things. The parables, recorded in both Matthew and Luke, begin with a story about a lost sheep. There were ninety-nine tended sheep, but the shepherd left them to find the one that was lost. Then Jesus moves on to a story involving something more valuable: a lost coin. Married women of that day apparently wore a garland of ten expensive coins. Jesus tells this second story about a woman who lost one of the drachmas and was anxious until she found it. Finally, Jesus ups the ante and tells his listeners about the most expensive thing of all: a lost person. This parable shows the heart of God for the lost in order to move the heart of God's people.

As Christians begin to think about their relationship to God and to his redemptive plans, they must not only have a passion for God's Word, but a passion for God's world—a passion for the lost. God will not allow his people to get by with merely quoting Scripture and the catechism. The heart of our Father begs for his own creation, even when that creation is in rebellion against him. And he is calling each of us to reflect his loving heart in our relationship with others—as individuals, as families, and as a church.

There are several ways to approach this last parable, the story of the lost son. Let's view it as a play in four acts. The family is always the working laboratory for matters of the soul, so the Lord sets his story in the context of familial relationships. A triangular power play is going on in this family. There is a wayward son, a warmhearted father, and a hard-hearted older brother. There is also a surprising ending.

Act I—The Wayward Son

The rebellious son departs from home. He not only departs from his home and family, but makes a huge scene. Had he waited, he would have inherited a great estate; however, he impetuously demanded that he have all of it at once. Isn't sin like that? The sinner wants it all now and will throw away relationships and everything else to get what he wants.

It would be reasonable to expect that the father would protest and say to the younger son, "Think about what you are asking for!" Another more likely response would be, "I'm not giving you anything, boy!" And the elder brother might have advanced this issue. But here we read a story about both a rebel and a father's wise approach to parenting his rebellious son: he allows the son to go his own way. Scripture indicates that, while he is the younger of the two sons, he is mature enough to make decisions and to bear the consequences of his decisions. Whatever rearing his father had given him—and in the story Jesus makes the father above reproach—he allows his son to work out that rearing in the context of his own heart's desires. So the father actually gives him his portion of the estate, and the young man leaves.

Dear reader, are you "cashing in" on the Father's goodness? Are you spending it all now? If so, your heart is set on the things of this world. You are enjoying the Father's goodness in so many ways—the pleasures of life that God (whom you refuse to recognize) has so lavishly provided for you. But note something in this passage. Jesus calls this kind of living "squandering." "Not many days later, the younger son gathered all he had and took a journey into a far country, and there he squandered his property in reckless living" (Luke 15:13 ESV).

Your life of rejecting your Father by enjoying his world will soon be over. One day you will come to see that you squandered opportunity after opportunity to come to Christ and be saved. Having wasted your opportunities, you will stand before God to be judged. Your temporary pleasures will be replaced by ruin in this life and eternal damnation in the next. What a wasted life and a wasted eternity!

Back to our story: this son came to recognize his sin. Jesus tells his listeners, "And he arose and came to his father" (Luke 15:20 ESV).

Do you need to follow the example of this son? Arise in your heart of hearts, see your condition, and accept the loving arms of your God, who bids you, "Come now, and let us reason together, saith the LORD: though your sins be as scarlet, they shall be as white as snow; though they be red like crimson, they shall be as wool" (Isa. 1:18 KJV). This is the Savior, who says, "Come unto me, all ye that labour and are heavy laden, and I will give you rest" (Matt. 11:28 KJV).

Act I, like the stories of all sinners saved by grace, is about a son who squanders his father's goodness but returns to his father in repentance.

Act II—The Warmhearted Father

The father never lost interest in that lost son. Yes, the young man had clearly taken advantage of him. Yes, he had an elder son who was loyal to him. Yes, he probably shouldn't have cared. But Jesus reveals the true heart of this hurting dad: "But while he was still a long way off, his father saw him and felt compassion, and ran and embraced him and kissed him" (Luke 15:20 ESV).

The Greek is rendered even clearer by the translation of William Hendriksen: "While he was still a long way off, his father saw him, and his heart went out to him. The father ran, threw his arms around his son's neck, and kissed him fervently."[3]

The father was waiting and watching for his boy. The father pitied his wayward son who had repented.

Jesus might have startled his hearers by saying that the father "ran" to his son, because running was not considered honorable for an older, wealthy man like the man in the parable. Yet the love of the father for his wayward son coming home was so great that his joy was boundless and could not be contained by conventions of behavior. The hugging and kissing brought a sad story to a joyful conclusion.

Look carefully, so you may see something beautiful in this text. Luke 15:18–19 reveals what the son had intended to say: "I will arise and go to my father, and will say to him, 'Father, I have sinned against heaven and before you. . . . Make me like one of your hired servants.' " But in Luke 15:21, he couldn't say it—he wanted to, but his father never gave him a chance to finish his statement. Instead, he called his servants to kill the fatted calf and ordered festivities in honor of his son—the son who had come home.

If you cannot see the heart of God in this, then you are missing the point of Jesus' depiction of the father. Jesus is showing that the heart of God is beating with passion for repentant sinners. And God doesn't make sinners grovel in front of him. No! The Lord treats us as joyful treasures reclaimed.

That is good news to any of you who have been living apart from God. Return home by repentance and faith. God is a God of love. Don't stay away fearing that he will beat you. On the contrary, he will embrace you.

The second act in the story concludes with these words: "And they began to celebrate" (Luke 15:24 ESV).

Now let's turn our attention to another theme of the story: the petulant elder brother.

Act III—The Hard-hearted Brother

"Now his older son" is a phrase that marks a change in the story. Jesus could have ended the story with a homecoming party. But the Lord was teaching in the presence of the scribes and Pharisees, as well as self-interested disciples and prejudiced crowds. The Lord was going to do some serious open-heart surgery with this second part of the parable.

Note the scene and the elder brother's reaction to the return of his rebellious brother and to his father's acceptance of the boy.

His hard-heartedness is shown by what occupies his time. The elder brother is in the field. Jesus positions the father in the story so that he can see his wayward boy trudging home

48

from a great distance. On the other hand, the older brother is placed out in the field, unconcerned for his younger sibling and consumed with his own thoughts. While our initial sympathies might lie with the elder brother, his location and emotional reactions show that he is not grieving over a lost brother. He is consumed with hardness and self-interest.

Beloved, what occupies your time? What about your church? Christians become hard-hearted toward the lost when they think that other things are more important than looking out for the lost. Work must go on, yes. But our hearts must ever be beating in rhythm with the Father's heart for his lost sheep.

Samuel Shoemaker was rector of Calvary Episcopal Church, New York City, from 1924 to 1952.[4] Shoemaker had a heart for the downtrodden, the lost, and the broken. This man, who was instrumental in founding Alcoholics Anonymous, determined to order his life and ministry so as to reach people who were without Jesus Christ. Read the concluding lines of a famous poem he wrote, "So I Stay Near the Door":

I stay near the door.
I admire the people who go way in.
But I wish they would not forget how it was
Before they got in. Then they would be able to help
The people who have not yet even found the door,
Or the people who want to run away again from God.
You can go in too deeply, and stay in too long,
And forget the people outside the door.
As for me, I shall take my old accustomed place,
Near enough to God to hear Him, and know He is there,
But not so far from men as not to hear them,
And remember they are there, too.

Where? Outside the door—
Thousands of them, millions of them.
But—more important for me—
One of them, two of them, ten of them,
Whose hands I am intended to put on the latch.
So I shall stand by the door and wait
For those who seek it.
"I had rather be a door-keeper . . ."
So I stand by the door.[5]

That older brother wasn't a doorkeeper; he was a door jammer. And the lesson of this part of the story is that a hard heart is in desperate need of repair.

The petulant brother's hard-heartedness also shows that he had no expectation of his brother coming home. The sound of music and celebration catch him off guard. It never occurs to him that his brother might have come home.

Do you approach Sunday worship anticipating that God might save someone that day? Do you go about your daily duties expecting that an old sinner in your community might be a candidate for eternal life? You will miss much joy if you shortchange God's power and his desire to save sinners.

The hard-heartedness of the elder brother is further revealed by his accusation of his younger brother and his flagrant self-promotion. The elder brother can't believe that his father is delighted to have the younger son home. In fact, the elder brother, Jesus tells us, is angry. His heart is so hard and so cold toward the lost brother that he literally chastises his father.

The elder brother actually sins in his response, as he tells his father, "All these years I have served you." He has served his father? Yes, he has done what was expected of him, but has never given his father his heart. That's why he cannot bring himself to celebrate. Since he refuses to join with his father to celebrate the return of their wayward family member, it becomes clear that he has been serving himself all these years.

He says he has never sinned. He is a liar. The scribes, too, boasted of their flawless observance of the law. But in this part of the story, Jesus demonstrates that all are sinners before God. The elder brother says that his dad has never given him a feast. He is ungrateful. Does not the owner do what he wills with his own possessions? Then, finally, he sins in not loving his own brother. He talks to his father about "this son of yours"—not "my brother."

You see, beloved, how a hard-hearted believer can act. He is so unconcerned about the lost that when one gets saved, he becomes jealous, gets angry, and sins before his father.

Do you see yourself in this story? Do you look down on the unsaved man or woman and think how much better you are than they? If you do, when the lost come to Christ and are welcomed into your fellowship still smelling like a pigpen, you won't approve. But the Father doesn't approve of that attitude. You see, a hard-hearted believer is a Christian whose heart is not concerned with the lost. And that is sinning before our heavenly Father. This is Jesus' point.

Now we come to the final dramatic act. Will the father body slam that petulant boy and teach him a thing or two? Read on.

Act IV—The Surprise Ending: The Divine Treatment of a Hard Heart

In a surprising twist to the story, the tenderness of the father toward his lost son is repeated toward his hard-hearted older son. In Luke 15:31, he reminds him that he has a place beside him: "All that I have is yours." And he overrides his son's objections to celebrating. He gently responds, "It was right that we should make merry and be glad."

In this tender moment, Jesus extends his love even to hard-hearted Pharisees. The Lord is calling such people from a dry, dead religion to a living, loving, joyful faith—a faith that is passionate for others to experience the grace of the Lord, just as we have.

The father explains the reason for his joy: "For your brother [and this is an answer to "this son of yours"] was dead and is alive again, and was lost and is found" (Luke 15:32).

The Lord has made his point. Do you see it? William Hendriksen explains that it is a simple message: "The central theme is, . . . 'The Father's Yearning Love for the Lost.' "[6]

That is the heart of the matter. How are you doing? How is your heart beating?

The parable of the lost son makes us ask: Is God's passion your passion? Does your heart beat in time with your Father's? There is a gospel recall on faulty hearts. Examine yours to see if it needs repair work.

Questions for Reflection

1. Consider your church's attitude toward non-Christians. Has your church forgotten the "people outside the door"? Are you avoiding these people out of fear, disgust, or hard-heartedness? In what ways can your church awaken to greater awareness of—and concern for—the unsaved?

2. How can you promote a spirit of evangelism in your church? What encouragement and support does your congregation

need? Brainstorm some ways to advance individual and church outreach.

3. Think of members in the congregation who have gifts of evangelism or a burden for unbelieving friends, family, or coworkers. How can the church lend them further support? How can you encourage them to encourage others to witness boldly?

4. Do you come to church each Sunday believing that God can work great changes in people's hearts? How should this attitude change your prayers and preparation?

5. Examine your heart. In what ways are you squandering the opportunities God has given you? In what ways are you hard-hearted toward God and others? How must the gospel change you?

Prayer

Thank you, O Lord, for showing us that it is not too late for a sinner to return to the heavenly Father, not too late for the grace of Christ to do its blessed work of redemption and restoration. Forgive me when I selfishly hold on to my place at your side, failing to open the door for more sinners to come to know you and your marvelous love. Thank you that it is not too late for my heart to be repaired, for my heart to beat with yours for the lost. I pray with humility, and I pray for Jesus' sake. Amen.

4

Value the Heart of the Gospel

A Commitment to God's Grace

GALATIANS 2:11–21; ACTS 15:1–11

Nothing whatever pertaining to godliness and real holiness can be accomplished without grace. —*Augustine of Hippo*[1]

"PEACE AT ANY PRICE" was never the motto of the early church. Indeed, in Galatians 2 and Acts 15, we see two different accounts of the same problem. The Galatians account is told by Paul, and the Acts account is told by Luke. Both accounts clearly reveal that there are some things in the gospel that must never be compromised.

Here is the heart of the matter: as you begin to seek a biblical vision for your church, make a commitment to God's grace as the preeminent and all-pervasive core value of the church.

Doing the Pharisee Shuffle

Once there was a very devout Quaker who, one night, heard a noise coming from within his house. He grabbed the shotgun that he kept hidden, so his friends, fellow pacifists, would never see it. He crept in to find a burglar in his house. He shouted at the man, "Friend, I would do thee no harm for the world, but thou art standing in the exact spot where I aim to shoot!"

Does this sound ridiculous? It is. It is legalism. Legalism, the theological idea of earning God's favor by doing certain things or following certain rules, always backfires. In the case of the Quaker, his effort to please God by his pacifism got all tangled up with his need to defend his life and property. So he did what all legalists ultimately do. He did the Pharisee shuffle, a favorite dance of those religious leaders who were "blind guides, who strain out a gnat and swallow a camel" (Matt. 23:24).

Have you ever done the Pharisee shuffle in your life? Have you tried to impress God and others by what you do, how you perform? Can't keep up with your own rules? Most people can't. Typically, legalism and hypocrisy go hand in hand.

In Acts 15, a controversy broke out when certain parties in the church demanded that new converts to Christ follow the Old Testament ceremonial laws of the Jews. Paul and Barnabas defended the converts, but the matter was appealed to the mother church at Jerusalem. Another account of this incident is related in Galatians 2, where Paul fills in Luke's narrative in Acts 15. Paul relates that at one time even Peter stood on the side of the Pharisees, requiring the Jewish ceremonial practice of circumcision. But Paul stood up to Peter in Antioch as he did to the Council of Jerusalem, and "the apostle of the heart set free" (as F. F. Bruce called Paul) [2] appealed to the doctrine of grace. Peter subsequently yielded to Paul (and to the Lord), and Luke's narrative picks up at that point. Peter then led the charge at Jerusalem and advanced salvation through grace alone, not through any law. In fact, he asked them, "Why do you test God by putting a yoke on the neck of the disciples which neither our fathers nor we were able to bear?" (Acts 15:10).

Yet this passage is *not* simply about circumcision and the ceremonial law. It is about our ever-present, sinful propensity to return to legalism, to revert to the internal default setting that looks to our accomplishments and our righteousness, rather than relying solely on God's provision in Christ to justify us. This man-made religion of legalism is dangerous to the gospel and to our own souls, as well as being an affront to the God of grace.

As you forge a vision for your leadership and pastorate, go to God's Word, where the Lord is calling you to cultivate a commitment to the doctrine of grace.

There are two great truths in these passages: (1) There is a continuing threat to undermine grace. (2) Constant vigilance is needed to promote grace.

Let's first consider the meaning of grace.

The Meaning of Grace

What is grace? What is this doctrine that occupies so much of the New Testament? Many Christians don't really understand grace, reducing it to some sort of religious feeling. D. James Kennedy used an acrostic to explain the doctrine of grace. G-R-A-C-E: God's Riches At Christ's Expense. God's grace is all about God doing for mankind what we could not do for ourselves. And this grace sets us free.

In the Old Testament, you see a God who promises that he will bring forth one who will crush the Evil One. When Abraham offered his only son as a sacrifice, the angel of the Lord stopped him and promised that God would provide the lamb. In the New Testament, you learn about salvation by God's love and power, not by the will of the flesh. Paul teaches that we are saved by grace alone through faith and not by works. Thus, in all of its parts, the Bible stresses the inability of humankind to save itself. The plan of almighty God to reach down in love and save us is central to everything we do. It is all based upon what we find in God's Word: God making a sacred pledge with himself to save mankind in their sins and offering forgiveness of sins and eternal life to all who will turn in faith to his gift of grace through Jesus.

An active, dedicated, hard-working church member dreamed that he passed away after a long and satisfying life. As he approached the pearly gates, he noticed a sign posted which read, "ENTRANCE REQUIREMENT: 1000 POINTS." He looked worried. He walked up to the angel guarding the entrance into heaven and said, "That requirement seems pretty high. Do you think I could possibly have accumulated that many points?" The angel kindly replied, "Well, why don't you tell me what you have done, and we will see how many points you have." "Okay," the man said enthusiastically. "I have been doing things for God for thirty-two years, and I had a perfect Sunday school attendance record for fourteen straight years. Also, I taught a Sunday school class for over twelve years." "That's wonderful!" said the angel. "Now let me see, that's worth one point." The man suddenly became very pale and began to perspire, but he went on. "Well, I tithed all my income, and sometimes even more. Also I served as an elder in the church, and I served on the finance committee and the building committee. I attended every workday; I mowed the grass and did repairs and painting. At every church dinner, I helped set up the chairs and tables and then stayed late and helped take them down. I witnessed to friends and family and won quite a few people to Christ. I never cheated on my taxes." The angel smiled sympathetically and answered the man politely, "Fine, fine. That's good. That's all worth another point. Now you have two." The poor man looked as if he was about to go into shock for a time, but he finally slumped his shoulders in resignation and said, "I may as well give up. I don't think I can ever be good enough to get into heaven. In fact, it seems impossible for me or anybody else to get in there without the grace of God." "Ah, now," said the angel brightly. "Now you're talking! That in itself is worth the whole 1000 points!" At that point, the man woke up from his dream. Although his bed was soaked with perspiration, he had a smile on his face and a whole new outlook on his Christian life.

As you read this, I am praying for you. You and I need to know that grace is the only way we can relate to God because that is his plan for saving us. If we are going to understand the church, have an ecclesiology (a theology of the church) that can pass a radical "Biblical muster," as Robert L. Reymond put it,[3] we are going to have to begin with church as "the grace place." Our good works are simply thank you notes to a loving God who, in Christ, did for our lives what we could never do.

So, accepting that, you can better comprehend the critical issue before the apostles in Acts 15 and then better understand the critical issue before disciples today. Does this kind of grace mark your view of the church?

The Continuing Threat to Grace (Acts 15:1–5)

The United States maintains a strong military because we live in a dangerous world where evil reigns and evil men are liable to attack. So, too, this passage shows that even when none other than the apostle Paul is preaching the gospel, there is the threat of legalism from those opposing the gospel of grace. In every generation, churches need a core value of God's grace.

There are always those who want to place conditions on what God has freely offered. "And certain men came down from Judea and taught the brethren, 'Unless you are circumcised according to the custom of Moses, you cannot be saved'" (Acts 15:1). In effect, these men were saying that unless the people adopted the custom of the old order (in this case, circumcision), they could not be saved. Simply put, they said that unless you adopt this outward sign, you will be lost forever.

This is absolutely abhorrent to the gospel. Why? Because on the cross Jesus paid it all for our sins, and his life is perfect enough without anything else! But these people are saying that Christ is not enough; you need our customs.

Legalism places a condition on what God has already done in Christ. It is a form of idolatry because it supplants the Christ of the Scriptures with a god of one's own choosing.

An attack on grace is an attack on the gospel itself. "Therefore, when Paul and Barnabas had no small dissension and dispute with them, they determined that Paul and Barnabas and certain others of them should go up to Jerusalem, to the apostles and elders, about this question" (Acts 15:2). When the free offer of salvation through repentance and faith is corrupted by legalism, it has to be dealt with. Why? Because that message corrupts the gospel: the grace of God in Christ is undermined, and the power of the gospel is lost. They stopped everything they were doing to deal with this issue.

The power of God to save is in his plan, not man's. That is why any teaching that adds any rule or regulation or custom or tradition to the gospel is wrong and will rob people of the means of eternal life.

Thankfully, this threat is always confounded by the unadulterated joy of those who have tasted grace themselves! "So, being sent on their way by the church, they passed through Phoenicia and Samaria, describing the conversion of the Gentiles; and they caused great joy to all the brethren" (Acts 15:3). Paul told the Christian groups in Phoenicia and Samaria about what God has done with the Gentiles, and they experienced great joy from hearing it.

By nature, legalists are not happy people, because they are always trying to win God's approval, which is a futile business and leads to bitterness, ugliness, and sorrow. On the other hand, people who have been saved by grace, who recognize that there is nothing within themselves that is good except Christ Jesus, are happy and joyful. Indeed, when they hear of another person who has found the love of God in Christ, they rejoice.

Jack Miller was a Presbyterian (OPC and PCA) pastor-teacher and founder of World Harvest Mission, one of the premier missions agencies in the world today. My wife and I once went through a conference with Jack. We listened to many stories that we will never forget. Here is one.

This pastor-scholar once counseled a man and his young adult son. The son accused the dad of hypocrisy, and speaking to his father in front of Dr. Miller, he said that his dad would never approve of him or reward him with laughter and joy. Dr. Miller interrupted the boy, thinking that he was being disrespectful, but the dad said, "He's right. It's all true, and worse. Let him continue."[4]

That dad's confession about his hard, legalistic approach to life brought healing, reconciliation, and joy into his relationship with his son.

Many parents who have tried to play the legalistic game in front of their children have had to face up to what their invariable hypocrisy produced: children who rebel against the facade.

Legalism brings sadness. It detests joy and happiness. Salvation by grace leads to grace-based living, and this produces honesty, openness, transparency, and boundless joy and happiness for you as well as others. You'll never find grace-based folks arguing over which tradition will save you. They will tell you: We are hidden in Christ. We have nothing of our own to commend us to God but our faith in Christ, which is also his gift to us. He has done it all. Glory to him alone!

Keep grace alive in your life. Watch out for the legalistic threat in your attitude toward your family, toward your church family, and first and foremost toward God.

That is not easy to do. Indeed, to keep grace alive, you must attend to this other truth in Acts 15:

The Constant Vigilance Required to Promote Grace (Acts 15:6–11)

In Acts 15:6–11, we encounter the Jerusalem Council dealing with the legalists' charge against Paul. We learn from Paul and Peter's defense of grace, that grace must be promoted as we do two important tasks:

Be vigilant to promote grace by carefully considering the biblical evidence for it. "Now the apostles and elders came together to consider this matter" (Acts 15:6). The fact that this council was held and that the Holy Spirit chose to record it for us today, shows how very important the defense of grace is. They met "to consider this matter." If you are relying on something other than the grace of God in Christ, you need to consider the matter as well.

When Paul suspected legalism in the Galatian church, he dealt with it right away:

> I marvel that you are turning away so soon from Him who called you in the grace of Christ, to a different gospel,
>
> which is not another; but there are some who trouble you and want to pervert the gospel of Christ.
>
> But even if we, or an angel from heaven, preach any other gospel to you than what we have preached to you, let him be accursed.
>
> As we have said before, so now I say again, if anyone preaches any other gospel to you than what you have received, let him be accursed. (Gal. 1:6–9)

For Paul, to oppose grace, to replace it with a religion that focuses on anything other than the finished work of Jesus Christ, is "another gospel," and he says that it is "accursed." In the Greek, the word is *anathema*.

So, to the idea that you can please God and earn merit by observing your traditions, you must respond with *anathema*. To the idea that you can please God through diet or dress codes or pride, you must say *anathema*! For you see, against these and every other legalistic lie, comes the joyous testimony from a great company of former drunks, prostitutes, prideful and hateful hypocrites, failures, paupers and kings, derelicts and nobility, Greeks, Jews, and half-breeds, all now robed in the righteousness of Jesus Christ alone and surrounding his throne in heaven. This glorious company testifies: "Nothing in my hands I bring, simply to thy cross I cling!"[5]

So Paul would tell Peter:

"I have been crucified with Christ; it is no longer I who live, but Christ lives in me; and the life which I now live in the flesh I live by faith in the Son of God, who loved me and gave Himself for me.

"I do not set aside the grace of God; for if righteousness comes through the law, then Christ died in vain." (Gal. 2:20–21)

Be vigilant to promote grace by faithfully defending the biblical truth of it (Acts 15:7–11). The apostle Peter, fresh from a grace awakening of his own, now takes the floor to advance the case for grace.

Peter's address makes clear four salient features of grace:

1. Grace is freely offered to all.

"And when there had been much dispute, Peter rose up and said to them: 'Men and brethren, you know that a good while ago God chose among us, that by my mouth the Gentiles should hear the word of the gospel and believe'" (Acts 15:7). Grace is promoted by evangelism, both corporate and individual. Acts 8:4 says that the early church went everywhere preaching! And what did they preach? Religion? No! The grace of God in Christ! And when you preach, always preach the core gospel message of grace.

2. Grace is applied by the Holy Spirit himself.

"So God, who knows the heart, acknowledged them by giving them the Holy Spirit just as He did to us" (Acts 15:8).

3. Grace knows no boundaries.

"And [God] made no distinction between us and them, purifying their hearts by faith" (Acts 15:9).

4. Grace resists human additions as it recalls human failure.

"Now therefore, why do you test God by putting a yoke on the neck of the disciples which neither our fathers nor we were able to bear?" (Acts 15:10).

A judge named Irving Kaufman presided at the sensational trial of the Russian spies, the Rosenbergs. His sentence of death for spying and seeking to provide the Soviets with plans for the atomic bomb was met with protests by Communists and their sympathizers. Judge Kaufman, in a *Time* magazine article in 1953, is quoted as saying: "I have seen nothing . . . to cause me to change the sentence. . . . The defendants, still defiant, assert that they seek justice, not mercy. What they seek, they have attained."[6]

Legalism—your own attempt to satisfy God's wrath against sin and his law's demands for perfection—has no right and no ability to give what God has provided for us freely in his Son, Jesus Christ.

If you are guilty of trying to please God with your own works, give it up, repent of it, and cast yourself again on the mercy and grace of God in Christ. There is no other way. If you have lapsed into the Pharisee shuffle of playing religion, of acting like a legalist, ask yourself, What better time is there to refocus on the gospel of grace than right now?

Conclusion

In closing, be reminded of this great affirmation of our faith from this passage: "But we believe that through the grace of the Lord Jesus Christ we shall be saved in the same manner as they" (Acts 15:11). There is simply no other gospel but the gospel of grace. You must receive God's grace and show his grace to one other.

For there is no other way to live . . . and be happy. There is no other way to believe . . . and be saved.

Questions for Reflection

1. Have your church leaders imposed extrabiblical requirements on each other or on the congregation? Are members of the congregation fearful of each other and careful to hide their failings? How can the church work to remedy this?

2. How can you be vigilant to promote God's grace through your conversation, actions, and ministry to others? Do you err on the side of legalism or licentiousness? Think about finding a trusted person to hold you accountable.

3. Consider the standards embraced by your congregation. Do any of these standards need to be graciously challenged by the Word of God? How can the church promote grace without encouraging some congregants to "continue in sin that grace may abound" (Rom. 6:1 esv)?

4. Meditate on the specific ways in which God's grace has strengthened you and freed you from fear. How has God challenged your hypocrisy in the past? How might the joy of God's grace change your congregation?

5. Examine your heart. Do you live your life in awareness of God's grace, or are you secretly captive to fear and guilt? How must the gospel change you?

Prayer

Father of grace, thank you that Jesus kept the law perfectly, so that I might be perfect in your sight. Thank you that Jesus endured your wrath on the cross in my place. I am sinless, forgiven, and righteous in your sight, not because of my goodness, but through faith in the goodness of the Lord Jesus Christ. I confess that I am inclined to trust in my own supposed goodness. When I do this, please remind me that your grace is the only foundation I have and the only foundation I need to stand before you as your beloved child. I love you! Amen.

5

Seeing Souls Safe
in the Arms of Jesus

A Vision That Is out of This World

**1 CORINTHIANS 15:20–28;
1 THESSALONIANS 2:17–20**

Those that sow and those that reap shall rejoice together, in the presence of our Lord Jesus Christ at his coming. —*Matthew Henry*[1]

HAVE YOU EVER heard a person declare that he wants to be a part of something that is greater than himself, something that lifts him up out of the ordinary, something that is simply "out of this world"?

All of us dream; all of us yearn for meaning and purpose. All of us really want to be part of something that is greater than the sum of self. In this text, you will get a glimpse, not only of God's great vision of the future, but also of the pastoral heart of Paul. You will see something that is simply out of this world. To get a biblical vision of the church today, you are going to have to move past bumper stickers and business plans, denominational aggrandizement and "who needs the church anyway" thinking. You are going to have to come face-to-face with the vision of a glorious consummation of all things. This is where we are headed.

Heavenly Mindedness

You have all heard the warning: "Beware lest you become so heavenly minded that you're of no earthly good." The message to Christians is this: don't get so caught up with heavenly thoughts that you have no practical effect in this present life. But C. S. Lewis contradicted that quote when he wrote in *Mere Christianity*:

> If you read history, you will find that the Christians who did most for the present world were just those who thought most of the next. The Apostles themselves, who set on foot the conversion of the Roman Empire, the great men who built up the Middle Ages, the English Evangelicals who abolished the Slave Trade, all left their mark on Earth, precisely because their minds were occupied with Heaven. It is since Christians have largely ceased to think of the other world that they have become so ineffective in this. Aim at Heaven and you will get earth "thrown in"; aim at earth and you will get neither.[2]

You've heard of churches with great programs, but which are essentially earthbound. You've heard sermons that are homiletically well crafted and even motivating, but are fundamentally of this world only. Indeed, many in our generation, in seeking to reach out to others with the gospel, feel that a more earthly message would be more "appealing" to the unchurched. Indeed, a great many of us have been living out our faith with our eyes to the ground, rather than looking up. Pray to God that your ministry will not be too earthly minded to be of any heavenly good.

You will see that the apostle Paul would have agreed with Lewis. Paul's heavenly mindedness influenced everything he did. And in particular, Paul's vision of a heavenly future caused him to be the kind of pastor he was and the kind of person he was. In 1 Thessalonians, Paul's words show that his present ministry is directly influenced by what he expects in the future.

Even under the weight of difficulty, Paul's vision always came through. As he recounted both the persecution of the Thessalonians ("For you also suffered" [1 Thess. 2:14]) and his own suffering ("who . . . have persecuted us" [1 Thess. 2:15]), the apostle Paul burst forth into one of the most passionate expressions in Scripture. The whole of it contains Paul's vision of his ministry. It is as if God has provided both pastor and people a glimpse of what a truly great biblical vision should look like. This passage contains two great features: a vision that is out of this world, but also a vision that is a blessing to all.

A Vision That Is out of This World

As you read and understand Paul's vision, you come face-to-face with this fact:

Such a vision gripped Paul's heart and soul. Note the language of Paul's vision. In 1 Thessalonians 2:17, we observe that he "endeavored more eagerly to see your face with great desire." And in verse 19, the heart of the great apostle pulsates with love for God and love for his people as he poses a question: "For what is our hope, or joy, or crown of rejoicing? Is it not even you?"

Have you ever been accused of "making the Bible boring?" If a man will simply unleash the truth of the Word of God, his listeners will come face-to-face with the most passionate people who have ever lived. Paul must rank at the top of those men with great vision, for he was possessed with a vision of the risen Christ. He was possessed with a vision of the growing kingdom of God, and he knew that his every step was moving onward toward the realization of that great vision. He was indeed a part of something greater than himself. And much of his ministry was spent explaining that vision of the grace of God in Christ and calling people into that vision. Make no mistake: this visioning message is not just for pastors or church leaders, but also for every Christian. We must convey the glories of the vision of the church. There is evangelistic power embedded in this ecclesiology!

A truly great vision must be a vision that is out of this world, because only a vision that is greater than ourselves can occupy our thoughts and dreams for a lifetime of ministry.

One of the greatest transformations in the life of a church occurs when pastor and people begin to forge a common vision. It is your work, as you follow in Paul's footsteps, to cast God's out-of-this-world vision. You must do that sort of vision casting regularly.

As pastor, you will be asked, "How many members do you have?"

To that you should reply, "Millions! We are a part of the glorious kingdom of God, which includes Christians from all ages!"

The concrete thinkers would then respond with something like, "But how many people in that million-member kingdom do you pastor?"

Of course, you will have to say, "None!"

But you want to cast a vision of the glorious kingdom of God! You want to lift the eyes of your congregation to the reality of the church of Jesus Christ. In the early stages of a church plant, the congregation typically meets in less-glorious settings. When preaching under a basketball hoop, for example, it's challenging for some worshippers to capture your heavenly vision. But if you are guided by a passion for the heart of God, a school gym—by the power and Spirit of God—can rival the most elaborate European cathedral!

My dear friend, you will commit a grave error in your ministry if you do not develop a heavenly vision. You are sitting among angels and, according to Paul, you are on a grand journey through time that will one day bring all of us face-to-face with the King of kings and Lord of lords. If you begin to see that vision, your heart will surely beat with the passion of Paul. Your life will share in this great desire.

When Paul casts this vision of people being caught up in the arms of Jesus, you are led to consider another place in Scripture where Paul works out this vision:

Paul's teaching in 1 Corinthians 15. In this great resurrection chapter, Paul offers a telescopic view of God's great plan that will one day bring all of us to a most glorious scene.

In 1 Corinthians 15:20–28, Paul teaches that the resurrection of our Lord Jesus set in motion a chain of events that will conclude with a great Resurrection Day. On that day, the skies will be rent in two, Christ will return, and the bodies of his people will be resurrected. On that day, the reign of Jesus Christ, which began at his ascension, will be unrivaled as every other authority, all other pretenders, and all evil will be extinguished by the cataclysmic in-breaking of his kingdom. Every knee will bow before him, and every tongue will confess that he is Lord (Phil. 2:10–11). Paul tells us in 1 Corinthians 15:25 that all enemies will be put under Christ's feet. And then, in the language of heaven, Paul ushers us into the far reaches of eternity. He tells us that as the kingdom comes in its fullness, Christ, having received the kingdom from the Father, will turn the kingdom over once more to the Father, that God might be all in all.

Who can claim to understand the scene? It is far too heavenly for our sin-affected mind to take in. But this is the vision of God. And your vision for the church must be subject to this vision. Hitch your wagon to what God is doing in his universe and be led by his Spirit. You will do yourself no favor, you will serve no eternal purpose, if you speak only of this world. You must begin with the end in mind; you must speak of heavenly things. You must lift up the vision of a victorious Savior who is alive, having been dead—a Savior who is marching through history toward a day when he will be crowned and exalted, and the glorious design of almighty God will be consummated.

A Vision That Is a Blessing to People Today

Now, returning to C. S. Lewis's thought, you can see in 1 Thessalonians that such an out-of-this-world vision is not too heavenly minded to be of any earthly good, but rather that such a vision always results in blessing. As you examine this passage, you will come to see a second great feature: this is a vision that is a blessing to people today.

Return to Paul's summary of the vision in 1 Thessalonians 2:19–20:

For what is our hope, or joy, or crown of rejoicing? Is it not even you in the presence of our Lord Jesus Christ at His coming?

For you are our glory and joy. (1 Thess. 2:19–20)

Souls safe in the arms of Jesus. Every great man typically has one consuming vision in his life. This certainly was true of Paul. His life vision may be summarized in this passage. He is saying that the vision of his life is wrapped up in God's vision of his great plan for the ages, and that vision has an earthly feature: he wants his people to be there when Christ comes again. Paul wants his people to be safe in the arms of Jesus.

My dear friends in Christ, this should be your personal vision for your ministry. You must be about the work of the gospel in your own life, so that when Christ comes again, your family and congregants will be safe in the arms of Jesus. There is no greater vision, and you must therefore work and plan and give your life to this great goal. Pray for your family and congregation, be a witness to them, and seek to live a life of faith, so that, as far as it is possible, they will be with you in heaven. Like Paul, you must align your vision with God's. But take care lest your vision becomes focused on yourself. No, dear friend, in the economy of God's kingdom, it is your work to cast that vision, to instill that vision in yourself and your family, to work and plan and give your life so that on the day when Christ returns, you will be there, safe in the arms of Jesus.

Hindrances. But be careful. There was satanic opposition to Paul's vision: "Therefore we wanted to come to you—even I, Paul, time and again—but Satan hindered us" (1 Thess. 2:18). Satan is not interested in preachers who are playing ecclesiastical politics. Satan will not muster the minions of hell against congregations that are playing church. But for a congregation whose ministry is about the coming kingdom of God in Christ, which is preaching and teaching that Jesus Christ is Lord, which is calling men and women and children to turn from their sins, to be free of the bondage of sin, and to yield their lives to this reigning Christ, there will come opposition. But greater is he who is in us than he who is in the world (1 John 4:4). Satan might have hindered Paul, but the presence of the church today is a testimony to the fact that Paul and believers then were more than conquerors (Rom. 8:37). You shall also be victorious if your vision is God's vision.

Conclusion

"For what is our hope, or joy, or crown of rejoicing? Is it not even you?" (1 Thess. 2:19). This is a heavenly vision, but it is a vision that is a blessing to people today.

Some years ago James Dobson, the founder of Focus on the Family, suffered a heart attack that nearly took his life. During times of crisis, a man reexamines all that is important to him and makes the necessary adjustments in his life. Dobson did this. He called his children to his bedside and told them that all he had ever taught them and done for them meant little if, at the sound of the trump and the appearance of Jesus Christ, he would not find them meeting Christ in the air. He tells the story with a quivering lip and a cracking voice when he says that he summed up his little charge to them with these words: Be there.

Be there. It's the most basic desire for any pastor. While you lead your church forward, remember that it is all for naught unless every member of your congregation is there when Christ comes again.

Will you be there? You can be—but not because of your own work or plans. Only through receiving by faith and following by faith the resurrected and living Lord of life, our Savior Jesus Christ, can you ever hope to enjoy eternal life with God. If you have never trusted in Christ alone for eternal life, do so now.

You may rest assured, on the very truth of God's Word, that as you receive Jesus Christ, you have entered into the very plan of God for the ages. God's plan for your life is that you glorify him and enjoy him forever, beginning right now. And he will bring blessing to your life as you come to know the peace of God which passes all understanding, as you come to experience the abundant life that Jesus promises to those who come to him. Coming to know Christ will bless you today, but the greatest blessings are yet to come. For his vision is truly a vision that is out of this world.

Questions for Reflection

1. What would make you feel successful in your labors in your church, home, or workplace? Would your life's work seem futile to you if you never achieved these successes? Look for Scripture passages to help you to reevaluate that mind-set and then commit them to heart.
2. Return to the church's vision statement you wrote at the end of chapter 1, revising it if necessary. Does that vision take heaven fully into account? Does it likewise reflect an earthly ministry?
3. In light of the church's vision statement, what should your own vision be? Write a brief statement for yourself

that complements the vision for your church. How can each member of the congregation embrace this vision on a practical level?

4. List the ways in which the elements of a Sunday worship service point worshippers toward heaven. How might these elements be better emphasized? How will heavenly mindedness ultimately help your church to be of more "earthly use"?

5. Examine your heart. Is eternity ever on your mind? How much do you care about the ultimate destiny of your family, friends, and neighbors? How must the gospel change you?

Prayer

Father, thank you for calling me to something much greater than myself. May my heavenly destiny inspire everything I think, say, and do. Father, work on my heart, so that I not only have assurance of my own heavenly calling, but also a burning desire to see my family, my friends, and strangers with me in heaven. As I encounter temptation to live a self-focused life, please remind me of the wonder of your grace. Thank you for giving me heaven as a gift through faith in Jesus. May I live my life in wonder and appreciation, for you. Amen.

6

Seeing Christ Triumphant in Our Generation

A Confident Vision for a Great Harvest

SELECTIONS FROM JOHN 4:1–42

> Do not give up hope for any sinner. Pray to God to save them. Let not any conversion astonish you; be astonished rather, that anyone should possibly remain unconverted. —*David Martyn Lloyd-Jones*[1]

THE MOVIE *Shackleton's Antarctic Adventure* depicts the incredible voyage of Sir Ernest Shackleton, who journeyed to the Antarctic with his crew during 1914–17. He courageously went where few others would dare to go. In John 4, Jesus does the same. He travels to Samaria. As he leaves, he surprises his disciples, the Samaritans, and maybe even you. If you are feeling like your life is a lost cause, or if you know someone who seems to be a lost cause, this passage is for you.

Winter Wheat

God delights in bringing life from death.

Traveling through the state of Kansas in the middle of winter, you'll see nothing but miles and miles of barren fields. Under such conditions, it's hard to imagine that you're looking at the "breadbasket of America." But what you cannot see is that under the cold ground there lie seeds, called winter wheat. Seemingly lifeless, but actually possessing all life, winter wheat germinates under blankets of snow. With sunshine, rain, and warm weather, fallow fields give way to glorious golden grain.

The principle is clear: God brings life from death. God brings seeds to life under frozen fields.

This is the way with souls. We can easily write off as unreachable and unconvertible those whose lives look the most dead. Have you ever done that? But God delights in bringing life from death. Reread John 4, where Jesus brings new life to a woman at a well—a woman with a checkered past. But even more, the woman is a Samaritan; that is, she is part of that Northern Kingdom of Jews who had apostatized by mingling with the Gentiles. She is a half-breed, a misfit, in the eyes of the Jews. In Jesus' day, as now, there was much racial and class prejudice. The disciples seem to dismiss the woman and the whole community of Sychar. But Jesus sees what others miss, and, in doing so, a woman is converted and a community is changed.

What would happen with your ministry if you saw things the way Jesus saw them? When you write people off as unreachable, aren't you selling the gospel short?

You need to see that harvest time is right now, that the post-Christian mind-set of our neighbors does not intimidate almighty God. Adopt the biblical attitude that anyone can be saved at any time and delivered from a life of sin and shame.

How might you cultivate this attitude? John 4:1–42 provides (1) a likeness to our own day and (2) lessons for your own life.

The Likeness to Our Own Day

Sychar is like America. Sychar was once an area rich in biblical literacy. Note Jacob's well in John 4:6. There were landmarks that pointed to a vibrant faith. Yet the people had, through sin, sunk into spiritual illiteracy. Jesus' disciples were not very interested in spending time in that area. But Sychar was of great interest to Jesus. He knew it was harvest time in that land.

This is exactly the case in America today. Our landscape is resplendent with the remnants of a once-vital faith. Paul Johnson, in his recent *History of the American People*, reminds us that the record of America is open for all to read and that it is undeniable that Christians founded this nation for the propagation of the gospel.

Whether or not you agree with Paul Johnson, you surely can't deny that churches mark the very landscape of our nation. America is, as De Tocqueville wrote, a nation with the soul of a church. America teems with remnants of a great faith, and that faith is in Jesus Christ. If you approach your friends and fellow countrymen with sympathy and with eyes of faith, you may engage some in a discussion of the deeper things of life, just as Jesus did with the woman at the well.

The main character at Sychar resembles many Americans. She was a woman living in sin, ignorant of true religion and of the great heritage of faith all around her, but she possessed some residual truth about the Messiah. Again, this is the picture of America.

George Barna has polled Americans and found some very interesting but conflicting information. A great majority of Americans believe in the divinity of Jesus Christ, but do not follow him. A great number of people know the word "God," but lack saving faith. How can this be? It is because Americans are so much like the woman at the well—living in sin, amassing a portfolio of pain through broken relationships, bad decisions, and living life in a rut without God. But many know something. They have heard about Jesus, and many of them have some decided ideas about him, albeit far from the testimony of Scripture.

You must reach these people. You must engage them with the language they have and point to the truth of Jesus, the claims of Jesus, and the demand of Jesus to be Lord of all.

The spiritually benumbed disciples are, sadly, like too many Christians today. Seemingly incapable of discerning the amazing harvest to be had in this "frozen over" land, the disciples first go into the city to buy food (John 4:8). When they return to find Jesus dialoging with this woman, they are amazed that he should be speaking "with a woman; yet no one said, 'What do You seek?' or, 'Why are You talking with her?'" (John 4:27). All of this underscores the thickheaded attitudes of the disciples.

Are you, too, guilty of this? It is possible for Christians today, like the disciples of yesterday, to draw lines between Christians and others—as if this is the unalterable case in life. Have you drawn finely crafted lines between them and you, and then withdrawn into your own evangelical ghettos to the neglect of the souls of those around you?

D. James Kennedy told the story about how he first came to share the gospel. He was out on visitation with a layman. They went to the home of a fellow whose language and demeanor shouted that he was an unbeliever. Kennedy nudged his companion and motioned that they should go. The layman asked the young minister if he could continue to talk with the man. Within a few moments, Kennedy witnessed the layman leading the rough-cut fellow to Christ. Kennedy learned that even those who appear the most unlikely are candidates for God's gracious salvation. He also learned the joy of being God's instrument to lead them into eternal life.

This was the way our Lord ministered to this woman at the well. He went where no one else ventured. He saw through the pain, the heartache, and the problems of people's lives. His gospel was more optimistic than the religion of even his disciples.

Oh, beloved, it was harvest time with Jesus in Samaria, and it just may be harvest time today.

The Lessons for Your Own Life

Never become spiritually desensitized to the plight of even the most hardened people! "They marveled that He talked with a woman" (John 4:27). The disciples had written this woman off (John 4:27, 31, 33), but Jesus optimistically seized the opportunity before him! Jacob's well led to a needy woman who was typical of the people there, and her conversion led to revival in Sychar (John 4:40).

Marcus Dods comments, "They must have been ashamed to find how much more capable an apostle the woman [at the well] was than they."[2]

How do you know when you become desensitized?

- You become unable to discern divine opportunities when they are presented to you!
  "But no one asked" (John 4:27 NIV).

- You become unable to discern spiritual things and are satisfied with worldly food.
  "In the meantime His disciples urged Him, saying, 'Rabbi, eat.' But He said to them, 'I have food to eat of which you do not know'" (John 4:31–32).

If you want to see genuine revival, you must be willing to go out, as Jesus did, to the hard places and the hard people. Do not let yourself become desensitized to broken, backward, hurting, sinful people. Instead, through your preaching and teaching, offer a glorious Christ whose life was freely given to any who would receive him and whose death on a cruel cross is sufficient to atone for any sin.

If you become spiritually desensitized to the plight of the lost in your community, if you possess just a little unbelief about what God can do, then confess it, get rid of it, and wake up to the glory of the gospel. There are broken, hurting people everywhere; find them, share Christ with them, and let God do his glorious work.

Never forget the powerful capacity of the gospel message! The disciples had seen Jesus transform water into wine at Cana, but didn't understand that transformed lives would be the greater miracle! But a woman at Sychar had encountered Jesus Christ, and she told others of her changed life.

A. T. Robertson, the great Baptist expositor, wrote of this passage: "So, he remained in Sychar in a continuous revival, a most unexpected experience when one recalls the feeling between the Jews and the Samaritans."[3]

This text teaches us some important lessons:

- The gospel has the capacity to transform lives.
  "And many of the Samaritans of that city believed in Him because of the word of the woman who testified, 'He told me all that I ever did'" (John 4:39). The Holy Spirit will take his own Word and find his target. He will move in places you never dreamed

of. He will stir and prod and find those souls marked out by God's great love and transform the hardest of hearts.

- The gospel has the capacity to transform communities and bring revival.

  "So when the Samaritans had come to Him, they urged Him to stay with them; and He stayed there two days. And many more believed because of His own word. Then they said to the woman, 'Now we believe, not because of what you said, for we have heard for ourselves and know that this is indeed the Christ, the Savior of the world'" (John 4:40–42).

In 1536, John Calvin had written his *Institutes of the Christian Religion*[4] and knew the power of the gospel, but he still lacked a personal vision to see the gospel take hold of communities. It took a persistent William Farel to draw him to Geneva and put his faith where the rubber meets the road. It was then that Geneva enjoyed great revival.

Can you envision a church that is on fire with the reality of the risen Lord, that tells others about the power of God's transforming grace, and that unleashes the stories of that grace to others still?

You will reap a harvest when you believe in a powerful and glorious Christ to save sinful men, even our own countrymen, in this Samaria of today!

Enter the harvest field with passion and expectation!

Jesus said to them, "My food is to do the will of Him who sent Me, and to finish His work. Do you not say, 'There are still four months and then comes the harvest'? Behold,

I say to you, lift up your eyes and look at the fields, for they are already white for harvest!" (John 4:34–35)

Robertson shows how Jesus' passion is seen here: "The Messianic consciousness of Jesus is clear and steady in verse 34. He never doubted that the Father had sent Him."[5] Jesus had a passionate understanding of his mission. The disciples did not have a passion for the lost, as the Savior did. They couldn't see what he saw because they lacked his vision, his love, and his heart for the lost.

The Lord invites you to see past the ordinary, past the expected, beyond the natural, to the possibility that God will break in at any time and change everything.

A seminary student tells this story of his hospital visitation: "I was visiting an elderly lady in a VA hospital in Miami. While reading Romans 8:28 to her, 'All things work together for good to those who love God,' a lady in the bed next to this patient was cursing under her breath, and she seemed confused and incapable of right thinking. She seemed near death and unable to reason through the gospel, so like a hardened disciple, I dismissed her. She then popped up and said, 'Do you have anything in that book that can tell me how to die?' Regaining my composure, I replied, 'Yes . . . and how to live now and forever, too!' To make a long story short, the woman came to Christ; she was transformed right in front of me. In fact, the woman was not only saved, but also baptized and discipled. Soon afterwards she died, a Christian woman with a great testimony." The student summarized: "I had entered that hospital room with no passion for that woman and no expectation for her soul, and look what happened!"

God is powerful, and his plans are immutable. *Believe.* Then, go with a passion for the lost and with an expectation for what God can do. This is *the vision* of the church that we need now more than ever.

Conclusion

In John 4 you have learned to:

- Never become spiritually desensitized to sinners.
- Never forget the powerful capacity of the gospel.
- Enter the harvest field with passion and expectation.

Martyn Lloyd-Jones beautifully summarizes the power of this passage:

> We tend to regard certain people as being "beyond hope," and assume that they must of necessity continue in their grooves as they are and die unrepentant and unredeemed. We just shake our heads over them and express our sorrow. We have talked to them and tried to persuade them. . . . If you and I are to save men and women, then indeed the case is hopeless. All our efforts will most certainly fail. But that is not our Gospel. It is Jesus Christ who saves! There is no limit to what He can do! His methods are not confined as ours are. There are no prescribed and definite ways where He is concerned. . . . Do not give up hope for any sinner. Pray to God to save them. Let not any conversion astonish you; be astonished rather, that anyone should possibly remain unconverted.[6]

It's harvest time—now and always—since the Lord Jesus has ascended into heaven and until he comes again. There are some imperatives for you because of this truth:

- Make certain that your attitudes about the power of the gospel are biblical.

- If you have never truly tasted of the living waters of Jesus Christ, repent and believe and receive the miracle of his gospel into your own life. He knows your past and your pain, and he offers you the prospect of a future you only dreamed of before.
- If you are a Christian, be comforted in that your lost loved ones are not so lost that our great God and Savior cannot save them.
- Pray for the harvest of souls in this community and in our nation.

Now, go and *live* a biblical vision of the church today.

Questions for Reflection

1. Which response to the gospel astonishes you more: conversion or lack of conversion? Are you astonished at all? How should you pray as you witness to others?
2. Have you ever considered yourself a lost cause? How does the Samaritan's encounter with Jesus encourage you? Think of a few ways in which you might spread that encouragement to others.
3. Think of someone whom you are tempted to dismiss as unconvertible. Why might you assume this? Have you assumed similar things of people who were eventually saved? Pray that God might teach you hope while using you to reach that individual.
4. How can God use your unplanned encounters with people as opportunities for you to share the gospel? Are you looking for these opportunities or are you spiritually

desensitized to them? Pray that God would open your eyes and ready your heart.

5. Examine your heart. Do you approach different nonbelievers with different expectations? How does this affect how (or if) you present the gospel? How must the gospel change you?

Prayer

Jesus, you love lost people. Thank you for loving a sinner like me and reaching out to me when I did not deserve it. Help me believe that no one is beyond the reach of your gospel. Give me a sense of enthusiasm for lost causes. Help me love people like you do by telling them your good news. Thank you that I matter to you. May I, too, love lost causes. Amen.

7

Transforming Vision

An Optimistic Ministry

PHILIPPIANS 1:3–14

Cling to Christ and live the life of faith in Him. Remain in Him and live close to Him. Follow Him with heart and soul and mind and strength, and seek to know Him better every day. By doing so, you will have great peace while you pass through the "temporary things," and in the midst of a dying world you "will never die." By doing so you will be able to look forward to "eternal things" with unfailing confidence, and to feel and "know that if the earthly tent we live in is destroyed, we have a building from God, an eternal house in heaven, not built by human hands." —**J. C. Ryle**[1]

HELEN KELLER WROTE, "No pessimist ever discovered the secrets of the stars or sailed to an uncharted land or opened a new heaven to the human spirit."[2]

While there are many pessimists in the church, today seems to be the day of the optimist. Is that Pollyanna attitude one that comes from a fleeting feeling associated with the installation of a new pastor? Well, read in Philippians 1 the Spirit-inspired words of a man who was locked up in prison, writing about the sovereignty of God and the life of joy.

True Optimism Based on a Firm Foundation

This book title may surprise you: *The Positive Power of Negative Thinking*. Author Julie K. Norem is a psychology professor at Wellesley College who writes that you can "harness the power of negative energy" to reach your goals. The promo for the book reads:

> Are you tired of always being told to "look on the bright side"? Are you criticized for imagining worst-case scenarios? Do you wish your optimistic friends would just leave you alone and let you be negative?
>
> If you answered yes to any of these questions, you may be one of the millions of people who have learned to cope with the pressures of modern life by using Defensive Pessimism, a strategy of imagining the worst-case scenario of any situation.[3]

There are consultants who advise clients that the church in America is not going to make it unless (1) we speak the language of the culture, (2) we determine exactly which kind of worship the unbeliever really wants, or (3) we develop the right marketing campaign, or program, or website, or on and on. And amazingly, in many cases, the solution is available from said consultant for a small consulting fee!

Are you discouraged? Could your new congregation be discouraged, given a change in leadership? Do not approach your pastorate with this attitude; instead, arm yourself with an infectious, optimistic attitude. Be more optimistic than ever about the future of the church of our Lord Jesus and about your life in the kingdom of God, no matter what you may be facing. Misplaced optimism would say, "Hang in there, you can do it." But your optimism stems from the knowledge that in more than two thousand years of human frailty, satanic opposition, and worldly attack, the promise of our Lord—that he would build his church and that the gates of hell would not prevail against it—remains as certain as ever.

Nowhere do we see this more clearly realized than in the early church. With an apostle in jail, apparently failing to evangelize and reach the Gentiles, the church's future seemed to be in jeopardy. But the truth is that while Paul was in prison, he wrote a little letter of thanksgiving to the church at Philippi about how God was using his situation to advance the kingdom.

From that wonderfully encouraging book of Philippians, and especially Philippians 1:3–14, look through the optimistic lens of the Bible to see that God is able to build his church through you. Truly, this is a divine description of an optimistic Christian and an optimistic church.

This description may be summed up by (1) the values of an optimistic church, and (2) the affirmation of an optimistic church. Both are firmly grounded in Paul's letter.

The Values of an Optimistic Church (Phil. 1:3–11)

The Philippian church had given Paul a gift—in fact, a gift of six values that can change lives:

Value 1: Honor the past (Phil. 1:3–5). The apostle Paul thanks God upon every remembrance of the Philippians. Their ministry had produced some great things in the past. They had helped other churches and had been a blessing to the body of Christ. Paul thanks God for them and for the fellowship they enjoyed in the past.

Remembering is a sacred act in the Bible, and is one that is commended by God. The Passover was an observance in which Israel was to remember how God had liberated them from an oppressive life of bondage into a life of freedom. The Lord's Supper is a commandment to remember—to remember that Christ is our Passover, that in his body and blood we have our freedom, and that we are on the way to our promised land. The book of Psalms is filled with the command to remember. In Psalm 77:11, David honors what God has done in the past: "I will remember the works of the LORD; surely I will remember Your wonders of old." At other times, failure to remember what God has done is sinful: "Our fathers in Egypt did not understand Your wonders; they did not remember the multitude of Your mercies, but rebelled by the sea—the Red Sea" (Ps. 106:7).

So it is right and good and glorifying to God to remember and honor the past. Remember that God has used the church that you have been called to lead in powerful ways. You may be sure that there are souls in heaven because of its past teaching ministry. Like Paul, look back and remember. Be thankful for the past ministry and for godly pastors who have walked through the hallways of your church. As you move forward in your ministry, do not disconnect yourself from the past. Honor the past.

However, you cannot live in the past. To do so is to erect a mausoleum and live among those who have gone before. In Philippians 1:6, Paul lifts the Philippians' eyes to the glorious present and future, and this is a second value of the optimistic church or Christian:

Value 2: Build for the future (Phil. 1:6). Philippians 1:6 is one of the greatest verses in the Bible. Paul begins by speaking of "being confident of this." God has done some great things in the past, but there are great things to come. The Christian life is dynamic, alive, and moving through history to reach each and every new generation that comes along.

Likewise, God is not finished with you yet. You honor the past, but now God is calling you into a future with him. And the reign of the Lord Jesus guarantees that he will see you through.

This is the heart that says with Paul, as Eugene Peterson puts it:

> I'm not saying that I have this all together, that I have it made. But I am well on my way, reaching out for Christ, who has so wondrously reached out to me. Friends, don't get me wrong: By no means do I count myself an expert in all of this, but I've got my eye on the goal where God is beckoning us onward—to Jesus. I'm off and running and I'm not turning back. (Phil. 3:12–14, *The Message*)

Value 3: Glory in grace (Phil. 1:7). A third value is in Philippians 1:7: "You all are partakers with me of grace."

The central theme of the writings of Paul is what God has done in Christ through the divine truth of grace. By sending his Son to live the life we cannot live and die for our sins, God has done what we cannot do. And he offers eternal life to all who call upon him by faith. This is grace, and Paul says in Galatians 2:21, "I do not set aside the grace of God; for if righteousness comes through the law, then Christ died in vain."

My friend, you are saved by grace, kept by grace, and your ministry must be characterized by grace.

Value 4: Abound in love and knowledge of Jesus (Phil. 1:8–9). In these verses, Paul shows that his own heart is for loving the saints with "the compassion of Christ Jesus." Then Paul says his prayer is that the love of the saints may overflow increasingly with "knowledge and full insight" (NRSV) to help determine what is best.

Value 5: Keep your eyes on the eternal (Phil. 1:10). Now look at verse 10. Overflowing love will "help you to determine what is best, so that in the day of Christ you may be pure and blameless" (NRSV).

God wants you to remember that you are on a journey, a journey of faith in Christ that is going somewhere—to the new promised land, the very abode of almighty God. Some of you will get there when we pass from this life, others will do so when Christ comes again, and all of us will see that great day of resurrection.

Encourage the people of God. Remember that the Word of God is telling us that the day of Christ is coming. How will you appear before his throne pure and blameless except through the righteousness of Christ?

Moreover, Paul is reminding us that we are on a journey. As we are filled with love and God's Word that gives knowledge and insight, we can live today for eternity.

Value 6: Practice your praise (Phil. 1:11). Finally, meditate on verse 11: "Having produced the harvest of righteousness that comes through Jesus Christ for the glory and praise of God" (NRSV).

Paul is saying that all of our lives are moving toward praise. The value of an optimistic believer is that all of his life is lived as an act of worship. Fill your worship services with expectation and wonder, and you will come to see that we are really just practicing our praise for heaven!

So, these are the values:

- Honor the past.
- Build for the future.
- Glory in grace.
- Abound in knowledge and love of Jesus.
- Keep your eyes on the eternal.
- Practice your praise.

As you, like Paul, begin to enact and cling to these vital values of the Christian life, it will transform your life and your fellowship, but it will also lead you to some insights and some affirmations.

The Affirmation of an Optimistic Church

The pain of our past is being transformed into the power for our ministry (Phil. 1:12). Cherish this passage: "I want you to know, beloved, that what has happened to me has actually helped to spread the gospel" (Phil. 1:12 NRSV).

The beatings, the false trials, and the imprisonments are not stopping the gospel but are advancing it! This is the truth of God's sovereignty, and it is for this reason that I am so optimistic.

Whatever comes into your life, know that God is causing all things to work together for good for those who are his (Rom. 8:28). This reminds you that if God is for you, who can be against you (Rom. 8:31)? This truth can be liberating and freeing.

What have you gone through in your own life that was painful? What pain or heartache or injustice? May you learn this affirmation of Paul's and be able to allow it to help spread the gospel.

The predicament of our present is being translated into a testimony for outreach (Phil. 1:13–14). Paul is saying that all the events that have led to his bondage have also led to his ministry. One who is not given to seeing God's ways might think that the church was sunk.

It looked sunk in the garden of Eden. But in Genesis 3:15, God gave a promise that a Redeemer was coming, and as the angel escorted our first parents out of Eden, a promise was already afoot. The predicament was being translated into a testimony of God's faithfulness.

You might have thought that the kingdom of God was sunk when an evil king in Egypt issued an edict to kill all the little boys born to the Hebrews. But God's faithfulness and his covenant were working through the predicament to fulfill his promise.

Maybe you thought that when an ambitious ruler named Haman conceived a plot to exterminate the Jews, the divinely chosen carriers of God's Messiah, it would be over. But in the book of Esther, surely an optimistic book if ever there was one, God works out the promise in the predicament. And at the ironic end of that story, Esther saves the day, Haman is hung on his own gallows, and the promise is preserved.

The predicament of Jesus' birth might have signaled to the angels that it was all over. Herod, a new madman in a long line of satanically directed beasts of the earth, sought to kill the child Jesus. But there was providence in the predicament, and our little Lord was saved.

What do you see at the cross but this same thing? The predicament was that the King of Glory was being mocked between two criminals. Jesus the righteous, the King of Shalom, was nailed to a Roman cross outside a city called the Holy City, which had turned against him. Surely here the predicament would finally prove to be the glass that is half empty! Here the plan would unravel and the Son of God would fail! But, believers in Christ, in this predicament came the promise! Early in the morning on the first day of the week, right on time, just as it had been foretold, the beam of divine power shown on the cold body of God, the man who lay dead in the grave rose up, the seal of the most powerful nation in the history of the world was broken, and Jesus walked out!

Because of this, my dear friend, because the central message of the cross of Jesus Christ is woven into the very life of this man Paul, he is able to say that the things that have happened to him have happened to advance the gospel. Like Paul, see the providential hand of God through your own predicaments, in the life of your church and in our great nation.

Our nation is suffering hard times. Television has become a pipeline for every sort of moral sewage you could imagine, and our people are being infected with a love of sin and are falling away from God. When the church gets a headline in the paper, you can just about count on it being a bad one: a bishop is ordained who is living in sodomite sin with another man, or a church is riddled with lawsuits because of shepherds abusing the flock. Our own denominational news is always filled with splits and falling away, with pastors in sin, and congregations railing against other congregations over petty things. But, my dear friend, in the worst times have come the blessings of revival. When we come to see that we have no solution, that we are locked up in a generation that desperately needs the gospel, we come to see that we were born for just such a time as this!

Whatever predicaments you may face in your church or in your life, say with Paul that this is working out for the advance of the gospel (Phil. 1:12).

Conclusion

Now, the gospel part of this message is not just to "be optimistic," but to follow the One who has greater plans for you than you have for yourself.

Here is a true story to encourage you. There was a boy named Toby who had Down syndrome. Yet Toby had a dream: he wanted to be in the Special Olympics and run a fifty-yard dash. Toby was almost thirty years of age, very overweight, and had asthma. But he clung to his dream. And he knew he could do it. The day of the Special Olympics race arrived, and Toby lined up with his fellow competitors at the football field; the gun sounded, and off they went! You probably would not have recruited any of them for your track team, but they were giving it their all. But Toby was so heavy and had such breathing problems that he fell far behind and finally just collapsed. There, lying flat in the grass, his tears mixing with the sod, his body heaved with disappointment. Then, out of the corner of everyone's eye, came his dad. You see, Toby's dad had a dream that was even greater than his son's dream. He wanted Toby to succeed more than Toby did. He wanted Toby just to finish the race, and for that to be his victory. He was even surer that it would happen than Toby was. So he ran out, picked up that big boy, and started running with him thrown over his shoulder. He started hollering to his boy, "You are going to make it, Toby! You will make it all the way, son!" Then

Toby got into it and started whooping and hollering, "Yeah, Dad! We gonna make it!"[4]

Think of yourself as Toby. You will be victorious, not because of a powerful, ingenious pastor or a hard-working session, but because of a loving Savior who is unwilling that any should be lost. He will see victory, you will be kept, and your lampstand will be in place when he comes again. This will happen because he wants it more than you do, because he promises to turn even your heartaches into rejoicing, and because he is strongest in your weakness.

Questions for Reflection

1. Review your church's vision statement. Will the church grow discouraged if it falls short of its vision, or does the vision place God's grace and your eternal hope squarely at its center? Revise the statement as necessary.

2. When Jesus instituted the church, he knew who would comprise it and what it would become. What can you conclude from that? How can you, as a church, continually keep your eyes on the big picture?

3. In what areas does your church excel in godly optimism? Where is it lacking? Make a plan for change. Which values do you need to emphasize more, and how can you best do this?

4. Does your church remember its past? Are congregants encouraged to share how God has worked in their lives? Are there any upcoming anniversaries you can celebrate together? Look for opportunities to rejoice in God and remember his kindnesses.

5. Examine your heart. What does your discouragement tell you about where you put your hope? How must the gospel change you?

Prayer

Lord, you are building your church today, just as you have in past generations. You can make a difference in the world without me, but you have chosen me to be your representative in this particular place and time. Let me not be discouraged by difficulty. Let me rely on you to work miracles. Give me reverence for your church, and help me see her as your bride and nothing less. Make my local community, and this nation, worthy to be called yours. In Jesus' name I pray. Amen.

8

Gathering

His Last Words, Our First Work

MATTHEW 28:16–20

My life is been flawed with many failures, darkened with many sins, but the thing in it which was good, which has enabled me to resist temptations to which I would otherwise have succumbed, to bear burdens which would otherwise have crushed me with their weight, and which has kept the soul within me ever joyfully conscious that, despite all appearances to the contrary, this is God's world, and that he and I are fellow workers in the work of its renovation—that potent thing, whatever you may call it, and however you may explain it, came into my life then, and abides with me to this hour—my one incentive and inspiration in this life; my sole hope for that which is to come. —*W. T. Stead*[1]

A VISION IS what you want to become; a mission is how you get there. Your vision must be born out of a burden for God's glory, informed by core values that include a passion for the Bible, a heart for the lost, and a commitment to grace.

You want to see souls saved, lives built up in the gospel of Jesus Christ—not only here, but also around the community, around the nation, and around the world. That leads naturally to your mission: how will you do it?

Any consideration of mission must lead every believer and every local church to the last chapter of Matthew's gospel and to the Scripture that must forever be embossed on the heart of the church: the Great Commission of our Lord Jesus Christ. It is the first great mission of the church.

Same Old, Same Old

An airline pilot once said that his work was really just same old, same old. You take off, you fly, and you land. No big deal. And most of us, when we fly, like that: the same old, same old. No surprises. No excitement.

The Word of God is life. The business of the church is the family business of almighty God. So when you deal with matters of our heavenly Father's heart and his program for his world, you had better make sure it's same old, same old. Charles Hodge used to tell his students, "We glory in the fact that nothing new is taught at this school." Modern-day translation: we take off, we fly, and we land. We deliver to you only what we have been given from God and nothing more.

This chapter examines a passage of Scripture that you have heard time and time again: the Great Commission. You will hear nothing new here. Any part of the Word of God, and particularly the very cornerstone of our mission as a church, should be same old, same old.

Jesus was born of the Virgin Mary in Bethlehem with a mission. He came to be our High Priest and to secure to God a great multitude of his own creation who were lost in their sins and separated from him. This High Priest received his anointing, his baptism, at thirty years of age from the son of a Levite priest, his cousin John. Then this newly ordained priest began his ministry of teaching and healing. For all of his life, our High Priest was without sin. Then in fulfillment of ancient Scripture, but in a surprise even to his closest friends, this High Priest offered himself up as a ransom for sin, as a lamb to be slain. His sacrifice for sin ripped the temple curtain in two, and our High Priest went into the Holy of Holies on our behalf and led captivity captive. He was in the grave for three days, but was raised again from the dead. God validated the priesthood of Jesus at the Resurrection. Our High Priest was seen by his friends and even by hundreds at once. Then this Jesus, before ascending into the sky and being taken up in a cloud, gathered his friends around him. The mission of our High Priest to reach a world of sinners was about to begin. He gave a final word to those who were gathered. That final word would become their, and our, first work. Thus, in the climactic last words of Jesus Christ on earth, the body of Christ that was left on earth came to know the mission of the church.

Given this scene, given that the last thing someone says to us is the most important and is to be remembered even more, you would think that these words, this mission, would forever be the main thing in the church. But too often you have to be reminded to keep the main thing the main thing.

Before you is a clarion call to mind the bottom line of the church, to keep the main thing the main thing, and the main thing before us is the very mission of the church of Jesus Christ, set by Christ himself in undeniable, nonnegotiable terms. You may have a nice facility, nicely ordered services, friendly people, and a meticulously crafted vision statement, but unless you mind the mission of Christ our Lord, you will become bankrupt as a church! So again, our Lord's last words must be our first work.

Now let us see what that means in this passage.

Our First Work Always Takes Place in the Context of Worship.

These disciples met to worship the risen Jesus Christ.

John Piper was absolutely biblical when he wrote, "Worship . . . is the fuel and goal of missions."[2]

The famous first question and answer to the Westminster Shorter Catechism says it all: "What is the chief end of man? Man's chief end is to glorify God, and to enjoy him forever."

We were meant to worship, and it is not accidental that the Great Commission comes in the context of worship.

In the worship of Jesus Christ, whether it is public (as in this passage) or private in prayer or in family worship, we come to know the very meaning of our lives. We were born to worship. We were made to come close to our Creator and to give him glory. The universal urge to sing, the universal need for a hero, the most basic human need to commune with this Higher Being, is all fulfilled at the feet of the risen Savior, Jesus Christ. My friend, it is here that we will find our vision and our mission for life, and it is from here that we must go out and bring others into the worship of Jesus. Worship is what it is all about.

Listen to the words of the hymn "When I Survey the Wondrous Cross." May the last line seal your heart to the "main thing, the plain thing":

Were the whole realm of nature mine,
That were a present far too small;
Love so amazing, so divine,
Demands my soul, my life, my all.[3]

Is your heart aflame for the glory of God and his will for your life? When you are convicted of your sins in worship, you are led to enjoy the very meaning of life in worship, and you find the very thing that God wants you to do with your lives in worship. Therefore, it is right that you should focus the life of your church in worship. In worship, the disciples came to understand that those who have been drawn to Jesus Christ are to go and, through their testimony in worship, draw others into the worship of him.

The very goal of God is that the ends of the earth shall come to worship the Lord. Just consider the Psalms:

> All the ends of the world
> Shall remember and turn to the LORD,
> And all the families of the nations
> Shall worship before You. (Ps. 22:27)

> All the earth shall worship You
> And sing praises to You;
> They shall sing praises to Your name. (Ps. 66:4)

> All nations whom You have made
> Shall come and worship before You, O Lord,
> And shall glorify Your name. (Ps. 86:9)

> Let all be put to shame who serve carved images,
> Who boast of idols.
> Worship Him, all you gods (Ps. 97:7)

And the vision of the prophets, likewise, was for the day when the mass of mankind would come into the worship of the Lord, for so Isaiah wrote:

"And it shall come to pass
That from one New Moon to another,
And from one Sabbath to another,
All flesh shall come to worship before Me," says the LORD.
        (Isa. 66:23)

The mission of the church was born out of the vision of God Almighty that every nation and tribe and tongue would come into the courts of the Lord and render him the worship that is due his name. The mission of the church was forged in the worship of Jesus on that mount before he ascended into heaven.

There, in worship, Jesus tells the church, "All authority has been given to Me in heaven and on earth" (Matt. 28:18). So now you come to understand that all of the prophecies, all of the biblical injunctions for the nations to worship God, focus on the person of our Lord Jesus Christ. He is the object of our worship, and we are here called, in the context of worship, to remember his will for our lives: that others must come and worship as well.

Our First Work Is Defined in Jesus' Last Words.

In this passage, three phrases define what we, as the church, must do—as well as how we must do it.

Go and make disciples of all the nations. This speaks of what may be called the centrifugal nature of the kingdom of God. That is, the kingdom of God is never to be stagnant, but always moving out. The nation of Israel was never to be an ethnic island of faith unto itself; rather, the faith was to go out to the nations. They were chosen to carry the Word of salvation by grace through faith in God's Messiah to the world. God told Abraham that through the covenant made with him, he would be a blessing to the world. Isaiah told Israel that their vision was too small:

> Indeed He says,
> "It is too small a thing that You should be My Servant
> To raise up the tribes of Jacob,
> And to restore the preserved ones of Israel;
> I will also give You as a light to the Gentiles,
> That You should be My salvation to the ends of the earth."
> (Isa. 49:6)

It was too small a thing for those disciples to stay in Jerusalem; God wanted the news of his Son to spread throughout the earth. And it is too small a thing today for us just to hear this message of God's grace in Christ extended to those who will turn to him; we must also tell it to others. But that is also too small a thing. You should dream and then work to take this message to our nation in this hour of need. But even that is too small a thing. We should go to the ends of the earth and call men and women and boys and girls to repent of their sins and turn to the resurrected Lord of life, Jesus Christ.

We are also told to go and to do it in a certain way:

Baptizing and teaching. We need to be baptized and taught. Disciples come in the context of a local branch of the universal church, and this speaks of the need for church planting, for establishing local fellowships ordered around Word and sacrament. This is the only way in which the church grows. This is a call beyond just witnessing one time; it is a call for the church to organize intentional movements of church planting around the nation and around the earth. We need to give and pray and work and go to help establish churches that will carry on the lifetime work of teaching. Jesus said to make disciples, "teaching them to observe all things that I have commanded you" (Matt. 28:20), and that can't be done in one hour. It is a lifetime of work that must be done in the local church.

Paul told the Ephesian elders that for three years he did not cease to proclaim "the whole counsel of God" to them (Acts 20:27). This means that, as a pastor, you not only need to share the gospel with your congregation, but also must study to show yourself "an approved workman." In other words, you and your family must grow in the things of God, searching and learning the Scriptures, and digging into the doctrines of our faith, all of which unveil the mind of God from his Word.

But to this command our Lord adds a promise.

Our First Work Carries Christ's Promise.

That promise is: "And lo, I am with you always, even to the end of the age" (Matt. 28:20).

When Stephen stood and testified that Jesus was the promised Christ, Christ's last words were his first work. He was stoned for it, but Jesus was there. When Peter was called to go and preach repentance and faith, Jesus went with him. And this same Jesus was there at the hour of Peter's brutal crucifixion. When Saul of Tarsus was called by Jesus to go, Jesus never left him. He who calls, comes alongside. When Paul was executed by a mad emperor, that great church planter, that great missionary to Europe, was not alone. Jesus was there.

When John Wycliffe was persecuted for translating the Bible into English, Jesus was there. When Luther stood at Worms, accused of heresy because he preached justification by faith alone and was threatened with death for that faith, he retorted, "Here I stand." He was brave, for Christ was with him. When a violent queen threatened John Knox with death for preaching the doctrines of grace, Jesus was there. When the great preacher Charles Haddon Spurgeon endured severe depression, agonizing pain in his body, when even his own denomination cried that his Reformed faith was antiquated and out of date, he stood his ground, for Jesus was there.

When our forefathers and mothers in the faith set sail from England, dreaming about a city set on a hill, shining forth the light of the gospel to the ends of the earth, Jesus was there. When the whirling winds and whipping waves of the North Atlantic cried out against their dream and told them that there was no way, Jesus was there. He was there when they endured hardships to found this nation. And when you take your stand in a generation whose mind is increasingly hostile to the gospel we preach, Jesus will be there. As you live your life, teach your children the gospel, and support the vision of your church to become an agent to preach Jesus Christ to this nation and this world in this our hour, he will be there.

And this promise, my dear friend, will follow you to the day when you are translated from this life to the next: "I will never leave you nor forsake you" (Heb. 13:5). This promise is our assurance. His presence is our guarantee of victory.

His last words remind us of one more thing:

Our Work Will Not Go On Forever.

Jesus will be with us "even to the end of the age" (Matt. 28:20). This present age will not last forever. Our mission has a sunset. Jesus Christ is coming again, and when he comes, he will call his church to himself and judge the world. This calls every generation of Christians to be watchful, yes, but also to be about our work, for soon the sunset of the world will be upon us. Soon the One who spoke these words will come again. And so, his last words compel us to say, his kingdom will go forward, he will save all of those given to him by the Father, and there will be faithful servants who will go. Jesus will not fail. His church will be victorious, though the gates of hell come against it. The real question is, Will you have had such a vision of the church that you were a part of this movement, or were you on the sideline? Make no mistake: his last words are now our first work.

Questions for Reflection

1. How do you live out Jesus' commission in the midst of busyness, discouragement, and earthly concerns? Think of several practical ways in which you can keep the Great Commission at the forefront of your mind.

2. Are you a faithful worshipper? Do you spend time praying and studying Scripture, or do you allow "life" to get in the way? What do you need to change in your schedule or thinking to make worship a priority?

3. Is your church open to teaching others, even those with only a basic knowledge of the gospel? In what ways can you make teaching clearer or more available?

4. Consider your church's priorities. Does the congregation gather on Sundays with the clear goal of worshipping God? Does your church act on its calling to make disciples? How can you encourage more zealous outreach?

5. Examine your heart. Do you ever think or act as though God has forsaken you? How must the gospel change you?

Prayer

Holy Father, we see from your Word that your goal is for the nations to worship You. Help us to catch that vision. Teach us how to live out your mission to baptize and teach, making disciples, wherever we are. Show us what this means for us in our homes, our community, our schools and workplaces, our city, our country, and the world. We want to live our lives to glorify you. Use us to draw the nations to you. In Jesus' name we pray. Amen.

Growing

What Is a Strong Disciple of Jesus Christ?

ACTS 2:42; 8:4

The more we grow in grace, the more shall we flourish in glory. Though every vessel of glory shall be full, yet some vessels hold more. —*Thomas Watson*[1]

BAPTISM ALLOWS new believers to take a public stand for Jesus Christ, and a good question for you to ask yourself may be: "What does God require now that I have received Jesus as Lord and Savior?" Well, God answers that question in Acts 2:38–42, as well as in Acts 8:1–4.

A biblical vision of the church today is not just about an idea, but about a life lived for Christ out of the abundance of grace received.

What's Next?

The Lord has shown every believer in the church what it takes to become a strong disciple of Jesus Christ. Indeed, his Word is given to us concisely in the Acts of the Apostles.

In Acts 2:42 and Acts 8:4, there are both instructions for a strong disciple and marks of a strong disciple.

Two Rules for Becoming a Strong Disciple

In Acts 2:42, we see instructions. The early church has been supernaturally inaugurated at Pentecost under the anointed preaching of Peter, and then catapulted out into the world. The trajectory for the book of Acts is found in Acts 1:8: "But you shall receive power when the Holy Spirit has come upon you; and you shall be witnesses to Me in Jerusalem, and in all Judea and Samaria, and to the end of the earth."

This power, given by God through the Holy Spirit, will now lift the church up and out of the atmosphere of Jerusalem and unto the ends of the earth. The beauty of the book of Acts is that, in a real way, it continues with you and the church today.

Have you ever wondered what it would be like to go into orbit in a spacecraft? What does the crew do as the spacecraft is launched into space? From this passage in Acts, you get an insider's view of the church as it is being lifted off. And what do you see? You see this branch of the body of Christ being gathered, and "they continued steadfastly" (Acts 2:42). The ESV translates it, "they devoted themselves."

There is only one Greek word used here, but two rules may be found within it.

Continue. First, you cannot be a strong disciple unless you continue. The early Christian converts were marked by their continuance. Peter's sermon was just the beginning of their lives of faith.

You cannot become a believer and just stop. You are justified so that you may be sanctified. You are saved so that you might grow. The very meaning of *disciple* is "one who follows." Following Jesus Christ is a lifelong process that begins anew each day.

A seminary professor walked into class one day and asked his students to share what God had taught each of them in their personal devotions that morning. When singled out, one fellow said, "Well, I didn't have time to get with God this morning." To that the professor replied, "Then you are too busy with seminary. You need to leave and spend time with the Lord first." He went on to elaborate that not only did their future ministries depend upon their continued time spent with the Lord each day, but also that, as a disciple, continuing to spend time with God each day is an unalterable and nonnegotiable rule for the Christian life. I know that story is true. I was the student! I was learning about ideas of Christ. I needed to learn Christ and to continue following him day by day. That is one of the best lessons I ever learned!

How well have you learned that lesson? Would you characterize your pursuit of God as continuing? Or do you see yourself as having arrived? In his unforgettably exaggerated way, the great Reformer, Martin Luther, gives us a goal for our personal pursuit of God:

> Let all Christians exercise themselves in the Catechism daily, and constantly put it into practice, guarding themselves with the greatest care and diligence against the poisonous infection of such security or vanity. Let them continue to read and teach, to learn and meditate and ponder. Let them never stop until they have proved by experience that they have taught the devil to death and have become wiser than God himself and all his saints.[2]

Note how a disciple must continue:

Continue steadfastly. The force of this Greek word is, as one commentator put it, "steadfast and single-minded fidelity to a certain course of action."[3] Eugene Peterson calls it "a long obedience in the same direction."[4]

Paul told the Philippian church, which was founded by the apostle himself, to work out their salvation with fear and trembling. Will you then think that you can follow Christ without such resolve? As Jacob wrestled with the angel for his blessing, so you should seek God's blessings on your life of discipleship.

The idea that you can be a nominal Christian is unheard of in the Scriptures. Disciples in the Word of God, whether in the Old or New Testament, are those who are strenuously advancing in their knowledge and personal experience of God. They have taken a stand for God and have identified themselves first and foremost with him. You cannot be a strong disciple without continuing and continuing steadfastly to follow him.

How do you do that? What are the identifiable marks of growth as a believer? This Scripture passage offers four marks; later in Acts, a fifth mark of a strong disciple is added.

Five Defining Marks of a Strong Disciple

A strong disciple of Jesus Christ is grounded in the Bible. "They continued steadfastly in the apostles' doctrine" (Acts 2:42). What is the apostles' doctrine? When Peter writes to the church in 2 Peter 3, he reminds them that the writings of Paul are in fact equal to the writings of the rest of the Scriptures. The apostles' doctrine is the body of divine revelation given directly to the apostles. It is in fact what we call the New Testament. And we understand the Old Testament in light of the writings of the apostles. In order to be a follower of Christ, then, you must be growing in the Scriptures.

A strong, healthy disciple of Christ is continually learning more about Jesus in his Word. He or she is reading Scripture and fellowshipping with a congregation that is committed to the Scriptures as the infallible and inerrant Word of God. Moreover, the disciple of Jesus will grow stronger when he or she sits under consistent, expository Bible preaching. This disciple will be seeking out Bible studies, Sunday school classes, and a personal devotional life that is consuming systematic portions of God's Word.

Martin Luther told his students something in the sixteenth century that bears repeating in this century: "Let ministers daily pursue their studies with diligence and constantly busy themselves with them. . . . Let them steadily keep on reading, teaching, studying, pondering and meditating [on God's Word]."[5]

You cannot be a strong disciple of Jesus Christ without studying Christ. It has pleased almighty God to reveal his Son to us in his Word.

A strong disciple of Jesus Christ is gathered in fellowship. "And they continued steadfastly in the apostles' doctrine and fellowship" (Acts 2:42). The early Christians grew, not only in the apostles' doctrine, but also in *koinonia*, that is, in fellowship. This is the second clear mark of a strong disciple.

A strong disciple must be in fellowship with other believers. We grow in grace as we are around other Christians. Since disciples are people who are following, they have not yet arrived. They are not perfect. Neither are you! Thus, when we come together, our fellowship helps us all. We not only need God, but we need each other. You might be tempted to say, "Well, these people can hurt me; they are not perfect yet and are liable to insult me or ignore me!" True. But the fruit of the Holy Spirit comes forth. The ordinary work of sanctification takes place when Christians living with other Christians have to go to the Father to ask for patience, long-suffering, and wisdom. Living with fellow strugglers makes us dependent upon God. Of course, it also encourages us, strengthens us, and inspires us.

Being in fellowship doesn't just mean eating together or being in the same denomination. It means being in Christ together. How does John put it in his first epistle? "That which we have seen and heard declare we unto you, that ye also may have fellowship with us: and truly our fellowship is with the Father, and with his Son Jesus Christ" (1 John 1:3 KJV).

The heart of our Lord Jesus pulsated with a passion for fellowship. In his great High Priestly Prayer, the Lord prayed:

> I do not pray for these alone, but also for those who will believe in Me through their word;
>
> that they all may be one, as You, Father, are in Me, and I in You; that they also may be one in Us, that the world may believe that You sent Me.
>
> And the glory which You gave Me I have given them, that they may be one just as We are one:
>
> I in them, and You in Me; that they may be made perfect in one, and that the world may know that You have sent Me, and have loved them as You have loved Me.
>
> Father, I desire that they also whom You gave Me may be with Me where I am, that they may behold My glory which You have given Me; for You loved Me before the foundation of the world. (John 17:20–24)

This remarkable passage shows that the fellowship of believers is based on the fellowship of God in the Trinity. Fellowship is often thought of in very human ways, but the biblical idea of *koinonia* is a deep doctrine that originates in the eternal past, when God the Father, the Son, and the Holy Spirit, in perfect fellowship, decided to create man to extend that fellowship. Man is alienated from God by sin, but out of love for fellowship with his own creation, God the Father covenants with God the Son to save this fallen race. Thus, the very coming of Christ is out of love for fellowship. The death of Jesus on the cross is for fellowship. The coming of the Holy Spirit from the Father and the Son is out of the love of God for you, my dear friend. Fellowship is, thus, an essential sign, not only of our humanity, but also of divinity. And God is calling you into a deep fellowship with your community of believers. But don't stop there, for he is also calling you to *koinonia* with believers throughout the world through the preaching and teaching of Jesus Christ as Lord.

A strong disciple is marked out by this commitment to fellowship.

A strong disciple of Jesus Christ is also gathered in worship. "And they continued steadfastly in the apostles' doctrine and fellowship, in the breaking of bread" (Acts 2:42). This phrase, "the breaking of bread," is almost universally taken to mean that whenever the apostolic church came together, they worshipped, and that their worship centered on the sacrament of the Lord's Supper, as well as preaching. Both history and the writings of spiritual giants who have gone before us seem to support this. But even if this means that the early Christians broke bread together in a fellowship meal, as we might call it, or whether this is a love feast (both Communion and a fellowship meal), we could easily appeal to the whole passage as supporting the concept of worship. Our Lord worshipped publicly in the synagogue. Whenever

Paul was visiting a community, he sought out the synagogue for public worship. In Hebrews 10:25, we are told not to forsake the assembling of ourselves together. A strong disciple should thus be a regular worshipper.

A strong disciple of Jesus Christ is growing in prayer. "And they continued steadfastly in the apostles' doctrine and fellowship, in the breaking of bread, and in prayers" (Acts 2:42). In the Greek, this last phrase says that they were continuing "in the prayers," which refers not only to private prayer, but also specifically to common prayer, or praying in worship.

A strong disciple of Christ is growing in his or her relationship with Jesus Christ in prayer. He or she does this in public, family, and private ways. In public, this disciple is attending a church where prayer is plentiful. In earlier liturgies of Christian churches, the congregational prayer was called the long prayer. But too often today prayer, as well as Scripture reading, has been shortened to the point of apparent irrelevance, even in Bible-believing, evangelical, and Reformed congregations. But our forefathers who were weaned on revival knew best. God blesses worship services and grows his people on large doses of prayer. In prayer we not only bring our petitions to the Lord, but in pausing from the marketplace of living, in going to the King of kings and Lord of lords, in acknowledging our need of divine guidance and providential involvement in our lives, we are transformed by prayer.

A strong disciple also prays in family prayer. Family prayers—those regular seasons when moms and dads and children (or single parents and children, or, for that matter, singles gathered with other singles when possible) gather to adore Jesus Christ, to confess their sins to Christ, to thank

God, and to bring supplications to the Lord—are important to spiritual growth and discipleship.

Of course, we are also told by our Lord to seek the secret places and pray, and this speaks of private prayer. Be a praying people, for in prayer you come to know who you are and who God is.

I love how Ole Hallesby put it in his classic little work on prayer: "To pray is nothing more involved than to let Jesus into our needs. To pray is to give Jesus permission to employ His powers in the alleviation of our distress. To pray is to let Jesus glorify His name in the midst of our needs."[6]

You cannot be a strong disciple of Jesus Christ without regular prayer in public, family, and private devotions. To quote Hallesby once more, "Have you ever prayed, 'Lord, teach me to pray'? If not, what, if anything, would be keeping you from praying that prayer?"[7]

A strong disciple of Jesus Christ is committed to witnessing. "Therefore those who were scattered went everywhere preaching the word" (Acts 8:4). Finally, a strong disciple should be making other disciples. In this part of the book of Acts, the apostles remained in Jerusalem, but the people were scattered. So when we read that "those who were scattered went everywhere preaching the word," the holy text is referring to the people of God—everyday, extraordinary disciples of Jesus Christ, not the ordained clergy. And this is important. People in your congregation will reach people that you will never reach. They will go places where you will never go. So it is your job to equip them for that work of ministry. Establish a ministry in your church that equips them to share their faith, that equips them in apologetics to be able to defend their faith, and that equips them in pastoral care in order to share the wisdom of the Scriptures with people who are in need. In short, make it your vision to see each person in your congregation "scattered" throughout the community, "preaching the word" in every circumstance.

Conclusion

So we have our answer. A strong disciple of Jesus Christ is growing in the Bible, fellowship, worship, prayer, and witnessing. In fact, he or she has now become a personification of the vision for the whole church; he or she is now gathering and growing and sending out other disciples.

In his book *The Legacy of Sovereign Joy*,[8] John Piper writes about the life of Augustine, Luther, and Calvin and their pursuit of God. He notes that all three of these spiritual giants were once nominal Christians—weak and vacillating, unable to withstand temptation, and given over to sin. But as they came to know God's grace and to see that God in Christ was the very thing they wanted most, their hearts were changed and they followed him, not out of legalism as before, but because they longed for Christ in their very souls.

My dear friend, unless you come to see Jesus Christ as your joy, you will simply be adding religious burdens to your life. The Lord invites you first and foremost to surrender to him, to receive him as Lord and Savior, and to see that knowing him personally is the beginning of a life of unending joy.

Questions

1. Reflect on the times in your life when you have felt closest to God. What might the Holy Spirit have used to

strengthen your devotion during those times? With that in mind, which marks of discipleship do you need to embrace more fully?

2. Do you have people to walk alongside you in love and friendship as you continue steadfastly after Jesus? Do they give you godly counsel, pray with you, and hold you accountable to the truths you profess? If you do know such people, thank God for them! If not, pray that God would send them into your life.

3. We need to be around other believers because of God's own triune community. How should this change the way you view the church? Think of ways to encourage greater community and fellowship in the congregation, perhaps through small groups, prayer meetings, and other gatherings.

4. Does your church equip its members with the tools they need to witness at home, school, and work? Think of some practical ways the church can assist its members in advancing the gospel.

5. Examine your heart. Do you want to grow in Christ, or are you content where you are? How must the gospel change you?

Prayer

God, I do want to follow you with my whole heart, in every area of my life. I am too weak and sinful to change myself. Please give me strength and desire to become more like your Son. Use me to accomplish your purposes in the way you have uniquely enabled me. In Jesus' name I pray. Amen.

10

Sending

Called to Be Taught—Taught to Be Sent
MARK 6:7–13S

Millions have never heard of Jesus. We ought not to ask, "Can I prove that I ought to go?" but, "Can I prove that I ought not to go?" —*Charles Haddon Spurgeon*[1]

THE GOSPEL OF MARK is written to people who are trying to figure out what makes Christianity different. Who is Jesus? And what does it mean to be his disciple in this world?

Mark answers those questions in his gospel. He often does it, not only with the word, but also with the way he presents the word. In Mark 6, for example, he shows how Jesus Christ answers the question, "What does it mean to be a disciple of Jesus in the world today?" The way he answers is simply amazing. He panels stories side by side, overlapping and interweaving them, until the careful student begins to see that the answer is hitting him over and over again. In this case, before Mark tells the story about Jesus sending out the Twelve, he tells the story of Jesus' rejection at Nazareth. Afterward he tells of the beheading of John the Baptist. Between the story of Jesus' rejection and the beheading of

John the Baptist, he sandwiches the story of the sending out of the Twelve. So the story goes from rejection to sending to martyrdom. The net effect is to powerfully press home the meaning of discipleship in the world.

A Great Library

Unfortunately, as some doctoral candidates move closer and closer to their PhD, they move further and further from God. Yet in many cases they are already pastors. How can this be?

If your love for research in theology is greater than your heart for God, you will find yourself in great danger. A story will illustrate this point well.

A learned pastor had just received his PhD, yet continued to pursue ways to refine his mind and discipline himself for the work of study and preaching. But along the way, he began to lose his vision for God and his true goal. He immersed himself in his work, as if research itself was the goal.

The Lord providentially brought him to a Welsh preacher named Mr. Roberts.[2] One evening, after Sabbath worship, Mr. Roberts invited the pastor and his wife to his home. Now Mr. Roberts was a very dramatic Welsh preacher, who was known for falling on his knees during the service and shaking the communion rail as he literally wept for souls to repent. He would often call out people by name, which he did with this pastor once, much to his astonishment. And like any respectable Welsh preacher, he carried a flowing handkerchief that cascaded out of his suit pocket. He came complete with a Dylan Thomas lock of hair that fell down over his eyes, so that as he stretched out his right hand to make a point in his sermon, he could deftly use his other hand to throw the lock back over his scalp. It was an ingenious move, very theatrical, and yet one got the impression that this was just Mr. Roberts and not one bit of acting.

Well, the pastor and his wife were having tea this particular Sunday evening when Mr. Roberts said, "You are a studied man, aren't you? I mean, all of this study here and in that doctoral program there with those learned men at the University and all. I mean, you really are something!" The young man did not know how to reply. The devil was blinding him, and he knew it. "Now," said Mr. Roberts, "I suspect that you would like to go to my study to see all of my books, wouldn't you?" "Oh, yes!" he replied, like a kid on Christmas morning, and jumped up ready to go. "All right, then," he said. "Let's have a look at my great library." They walked slowly up the old staircase in the manse, arriving at the top of the stairs, and went into the room he called his study. It was dark, and all you could see was empty shelf after empty shelf. The young man was confused. "Well, what do you think of my fine library? Do you think the boys at the University would approve?" He stood speechless, waiting for the show to carry on. "Well, look, there on that table, there are all of my books! All sixty-six of my books!"

In the middle of the empty library was a table with a Bible on it. Nothing else. In fact, there were no other furnishings in the room save a chair. "Now look here," the Welsh preacher said, as he looked the young man in the eye, "years ago, God told me that I was depending too much on books and study and not enough on his Book. So I got rid of them all!" He continued, "Young man, you must never allow anything to get in the way of trusting in the Holy Spirit and his Word alone."

That night, the young man learned that *he was called to be taught and taught to be sent*. I know that story well. I was that young pastor. I hope I never forget the lesson!

To have a biblical vision for the church today is to understand that we have been called to be witnesses in the world. We gather to grow in order to leave to share. We often share through deed—most popular today in mercy ministries (a most biblical thing to do)[3]—but never to the exclusion of preaching the Word. When I say preaching the Word, I mean in the way that the disciples were scattered abroad and preaching the Word everywhere (Acts 8:4).[4] The "clergy," as it were, remained in Jerusalem. But Acts 8 shows us that the people of God were run off by persecution. It is possible for people to think that they are Christians, but to miss the point. For this is a Christian: called, taught, and sent. Moreover, it is possible even for true believers in Jesus Christ to get confused about this essential character of the Christian faith.

The gospel of Mark brings you back to this basic message in Mark 6:7–13. The sending of the Twelve in Mark is, not surprisingly, the shortest account of this event, which also appears in Matthew and in Luke. In Matthew's account, we find the tremendous teaching about what it is to be a disciple. In Matthew's expanded story of the sending of the Twelve, we read:

> A student is not above his teacher. (Matt. 10:24 NIV)

> If the head of the house has been called Beelzebub, how much more the member of his household! (Matt. 10:25 NIV)

> Do not be afraid of those who kill the body but cannot kill the soul. Rather be afraid of the One who can destroy both soul and body in hell. (Matt. 10:28 NIV)

> Whoever acknowledges me before men, I will also acknowledge him before my Father in heaven. But whoever disowns

me before men, I will disown him before my Father in heaven. (Matt. 10:32–33 NIV)

Do not suppose that I have come to bring peace to the earth. I did not come to bring peace, but a sword. (Matt. 10:34 NIV)

Anyone who loves his father or mother more than me is not worthy of me; anyone who loves his son or daughter more than me is not worthy of me; and anyone who does not take his cross and follow me in not worthy of me. Whoever finds his life will lose it, and whoever loses his life for my sake will find it. (Matt. 10:37–39 NIV)

Reread that last verse; does it bear down into your soul? Is there shallowness in your profession? This is the context. Mark is giving you an account of the sending out of the Twelve, sandwiched between rejection at Nazareth and the beheading of John. In this you come to see what it means to be a Christian.

We are called to be taught, and taught to be sent. In this chapter, we will briefly consider the fact that a true believer must be called and taught. In addition, we will see Jesus' teaching about being sent.

A True Disciple Is Called by Jesus.

A true disciple of Jesus is a person who has been called by Jesus. He called his disciples as they were working at their jobs. In this passage, before they are sent, he again calls them to himself. Jesus calls us in salvation, he calls us in teaching, and he calls us in sending. A disciple is not a person who turns over a new leaf or makes a decision for Jesus, but one whose life is radically transformed by Jesus' claim on his or her life.

This is the uniform teaching of the Word of God.

> You did not choose me, but I chose you and appointed you that you should go and bear fruit. (John 15:16 ESV)

> The God of this people Israel chose our fathers. (Acts 13:17 ESV)

> He chose us in him before the foundation of the world, that we should be holy and blameless before him. (Eph. 1:4 ESV)

The issue is simply this: Jesus has come. His Word is in front of you, and he is calling you. Dietrich Bonhoeffer put it better:

> One thing is clear: we understand Christ only if we commit ourselves to Him in a stark "Either-Or." He did not go to the cross to ornament and embellish our life. If we wish to have him, then He demands the right to say something decisive about our entire life. We do not understand Him if we arrange for Him only a small compartment of our spiritual life. Rather, we understand our spiritual life only if we then orientate it to him alone or give a flat "No."[5]

You are here for a purpose, and it is not to fill space in a church—or, if you are a pastor, to have a prominent church pastorate on your résumé. Either you have heard the compelling call of Christ on your life and you are in the church as a member of the body of Christ or your presence there means nothing.

The essential character of discipleship is the call of God. It is the call of God in Christ in salvation. It is the call of God in Christ in discipleship, also. The men in Mark 6 who had been called to Christ were called to Christ again before they were sent. You cannot live the Christian life without coming to Christ again and again and again—not for salvation, mind you, for that is a once-and-always thing, but for guidance, for direction, and for clarification of our lives as his disciples.

A True Disciple Is Taught by Jesus.

We need to make sure we understand that a true disciple of Jesus is taught by him.

Matthew gives us more of Jesus' teaching just before his disciples were sent out, but Mark shows this in a different way. He shows us, dramatically, that before they went out as his disciples, Jesus taught them through the example of his own life. He was rejected. Mark doesn't record the actual teaching that went on; he just tells the story about Jesus' rejection right before the Twelve were sent. Mark often leaves it for his audience to fill in the blank. He moves quickly. But he doesn't miss it. They were called to be taught.

In many circles, there is almost a distaste for learning. It is as if to study the Word of God seriously or to inquire into the nature of God (what is called theology proper) somehow leaves one suspect. Much of this suspicion of learning and faith comes from seemingly faithful men going off to seminary to become godless liberals. But must one throw out the baby with the bathwater? Mark Noll wrote an outstanding book on this subject, called *The Scandal of the Evangelical Mind*. Noll began his first page with this statement: "The scandal of the evangelical mind is that there is no evangelical mind."[6] Now that is hyperbolic and disturbing, designed to draw you into the book. But his premise is that we have failed to renew our minds as Paul called us to do. Have you failed to love God with your mind, as Jesus called you to do? Have you forgotten that the Great Commission is to "Go . . . teaching them to observe all things that I have commanded you" (Matt. 28:19–20)? You are not ready to be sent until you are being taught by Jesus— not sterile, academic teaching, but sit-at-the-feet-of-the-Savior teaching. As a result, many have been satisfied with the hem of Christ for salvation, but have missed his deeper teaching for life transformation. Some proclaim a Christianity that does not contain the whole counsel of God and may not even be true faith. To be a disciple is to sit at the feet of the Master.

Are you seated at the feet of the Master? Are you deep into his Word? Are you finding time for authentic, soul-changing, heaven-pleading, Christ-saturated prayer?

A True Disciple Is Sent by Jesus.

A true disciple of Jesus is sent by him. You cannot be a disciple without being called by Jesus, taught by Jesus, and also sent by Jesus. Let us consider the three characteristics of this sending.

True believers, like the Twelve, are sent with a commission. The commission here is simple:

- Go.

    You must go. You were not called and taught to grow spiritually fat and sluggish, but to go and bear fruit. True believers are people who are reproducing their faith, teaching the teachings of their Savior to others.

- Go together.

    They are sent out two by two. This accords with all of the teaching of God in the Bible, for testimony is established in twos. Thus, you have Peter and John, Paul and Barnabus, Paul and Silas, and so forth.

Another minister once explained this sending by twos by saying, "The great secret to the pastorate is never to do ministry alone." Do not forget this. Pastors need other people so that they can equip each other. In other words, your work is to equip the saints for the work of ministry, and you should do that in the company of others. I believe that this applies in all of our Christian lives. The church is not a privatized institution, but an organic movement of the Holy Spirit uniting believers together as one in Christ and going forth together—not in isolation—to bring the gospel to the world.

The buddy system is used in the US Army. In the Air Force, as planes fly in tight formation, one pilot checks the wing of another. They communicate with each other as they fly. They keep each other on course.

Don't you think this is what Jesus is doing? You go into battle with a battle buddy. He looks out for you, he covers your back, he gives you encouragement, he holds you accountable, he sees what you see, and together you make better decisions.

Fellow believers, there is a great principle here. God has placed you on a team called the church. There are to be no lone wolves in the church. In Acts 2, after the great outpouring of the Spirit at Pentecost, the saints gathered immediately into local assemblies. Indeed, in the Bible the word for church is *ekklesia*, and it means "the assembly."[7] In the Old Testament, the word is *qahal*[8] or *'atsereth*,[9] and it is translated "assembly" or, as in Joel 2:15, "sacred [or "solemn"] assembly." In other places, the Holy Spirit used the Hebrew word *'edah*[10]— "congregation." Stephen, in his glorious sermon before being martyred for Christ, uses the word *ekklesia* to refer to the "congregation" that was in the wilderness under Moses, implying that it was the Old Testament church:

This is the one who was in the congregation in the wilderness with the angel who spoke to him at Mount Sinai, and with our fathers. He received living oracles to give to us. (Acts 7:38 ESV)

In the epistle to the Hebrews, the word "congregation" is likewise *ekklesia*: "I will tell of your name to my brothers; in the midst of the congregation I will sing your praise" (Heb. 2:12 ESV).

The people of God are not to forsake "the assembling of ourselves together" (Heb. 10:25). They are to "have church," as our African-American brothers and sisters put it so beautifully. There are to be no loose cannons in the body of Christ. Paul told Titus, "Set in order the things that are lacking, and appoint elders in every city" (Titus 1:5). That is plural: elders.

All of this speaks not only to a scriptural theology of the church, but also to a divine intention for the church.[11] The Lord means for his people to be gathered together in local fellowships under the spiritual covering of pastors and elders.

Are you in a place of covenant relationship with a few fellow pilgrims? If not, seek out brothers and sisters in the Lord and make your home among them—be it in a cathedral or a cave. The church is not a place. It is a movement. It is more, says Paul—"the body of Christ." "Likewise, my brothers, you also have died to the law through the body of Christ, so that you may belong to another, to him who has been raised from the dead, in order that we may bear fruit for God" (Rom. 7:4 ESV).

The church is our God-appointed home in this old world. One day we shall be gathered with all of the church—from Adam to the last one caught up in the sky—to be with the Lord forever, in a new heaven and a new earth.

• Go with authority.

Jesus told his disciples that they had authority over demons. Now, unless you look at the Bible with a redemptive-historical lens, you may be confused. These twelve were sent directly by Jesus. The word for *sent* in the Greek is the root from which we get the word *apostle*. There are no more apostles. But still, every Christian is sent forth with authority from Jesus. That authority is to proclaim what God has done for you. That is what the man of the tombs did. He was healed and delivered and told what things God had done for him (Mark 5:2–20). Peter says, "But you are a chosen race, a royal priesthood, a holy nation, a people for his own possession, that you may proclaim the excellencies of him who called you out of darkness into his marvelous light" (1 Peter 2:9 ESV).

Paul calls us "ambassadors for Christ," sent forth to plead with men to be reconciled with God through Jesus Christ (2 Cor. 5:20). And Paul speaks in Ephesians 3:20 of "him who is able to do far more abundantly than all that we ask or think, according to the power at work within us" (Eph. 3:20 ESV). Thus, we have Christ's power, and that is his authority.

• Go with authority over evil.

When Christ is preached in your home in family worship, there is power over evil. When Christ is shared in love with others, there is life-changing power that will restore marriage, give comfort in grieving, and translate a dead sinner into a living saint of God.

But there is more.

Genuine disciples, like the Twelve, are sent with a command.
The command of Jesus to his disciples involved how they
should go. He allowed a staff (a walking stick) and sandals.
But he forbade bread, a bag for supplies, money, and an extra
tunic, which would have been used for a covering at night.
In other words, they were to go and depend on Jesus alone
for the journey.

This may very well be the central part that many of you
need. It is certainly what pastors and church leaders need to
hear. Jesus is not sending us out with everything neat and
tidy. Christ is calling you to go, and he is showing you that
if he calls, he will equip, and if he equips, he will sustain.

As a minister who pastors seminarians and often teaches
among pastors, I call those who are called by God to think
back to the early moments of their call. I plead with them to
become reacquainted with that call of Christ—to "romance
the call" in their lives. This is not that dissimilar to when I
am counseling a couple having troubles and I call them to go
back to the special song in their courtship. Sometimes, when
I am particularly playful (or mean), I will ask the husband to
turn to his wife and sing their song! I have had a few laughs
doing that. But I have also seen tears of relief and renewal.
To study this book is to renew your love for Christ and his
church. It is to sing the songs of Zion again. Do you remember when you first sang "Amazing love! How can it be that
thou, my God, shouldst die for me?"[12] Let the power of your
encounter with Jesus Christ now move you forward in your
vision of the church. That song of the church becomes the
soundtrack of your own personal mission in the world for
Jesus Christ.

The Lord also told his disciples to stay where they landed.
They were to go out and minister from there, but if someone

took them in, that became their home base—their staging area, if you will—for gospel work. They didn't have to worry about this. Have you ever heard someone say, "Bloom where you are planted"? This is the place to support such a saying biblically. God will direct you, and you must stay there until he directs you elsewhere. If your message is rejected, then, according to Jesus, you go elsewhere.

In all of this, there is a sense of dependence on Christ and a sense of urgency in the gospel.

Faithful followers, like the Twelve, are sent with a communiqué. Mark 6:12 indicates that the message is, "Repent." Matthew adds, "The kingdom of heaven is at hand" (Matt. 10:7). And Luke sums it up as "preaching the gospel" (Luke 9:6). What is the gospel message? It is this: Turn from your sins, for in the coming of Jesus of Nazareth the kingdom of God has come to earth. He is here. This is the One. Look for no other. You are called upon to turn to him and him alone.

Mark 6:13 gives you the necessary companion to this first message: "Heal them." The anointing with oil mentioned in that verse is simply a sign. The olive oil could not produce the sort of instantaneous, miraculous healing that is in view here. The apostles had the supernatural touch of God, the power to heal and cast out demons. You do not have that power. But you are to bring healing.

Indeed, it is here that you learn a vital truth: the gospel must go forth in word and in deed. Not word alone. Not deed alone. One is intellectualism or fundamentalism in the worst sense; the other is a social gospel; neither is the true gospel. The gospel goes forth in word as you feed the poor. You feed the poor and also share Jesus Christ with them. The gospel goes forth as you comfort the grieving. It goes forth when you share the beauty of our Savior's grace as we minister physical and emotional comfort.

You are called to be taught, and you are taught to be sent. And you are sent to speak of Christ and to be Christ for a world in need.

Conclusion

The mission statement of your church should reflect this truth: disciples should be gathered, then grown, and then sent out as strong disciples of Jesus Christ. For Christ called you not only to teach, but also to share that teaching with a world in need. Do not forget sending!

A true disciple is called to be taught, and taught to be sent.

Questions for Reflection

1. Evaluate your church's ministry. Does it take a holistic, biblically balanced approach to gathering, growing, and sending? What aspects of ministry do you need to change or develop?
2. Reflect on your attitude to God's role in your life. Do you go to Christ daily for guidance, direction, and clarification, or are you living in your own strength? Are you relying on other books—even Christian books—more than his Word? How can you practice greater reliance on God instead of self?
3. In what areas of ministry does your church need to step out in faith? Do you have a specific vision for the ministry that God has given your church? How are you living in light of the urgency of the gospel?

4. Are members of your church suffering for Christ's sake? Think of ways in which you might encourage them. Does the worship service prepare the congregation for trials and difficulties faced throughout the week?

5. Examine your heart. Do you long to sit at the feet of Jesus and be taught by him? How must the gospel change you?

Prayers

My great God and Father, how good you have been to call me to yourself. Thank you for Jesus and the sacrifice he made on my behalf. I ask that you would continue to apply these truths to my life. Teach me what it means to sit at the feet of Jesus. I ask that you would grant me boldness as I seek to follow your will. Lead me, that I might be used in the furthering of your kingdom. In Christ's name I pray. Amen.

11

Expository Preaching

The Marks of Biblical Preaching

NEHEMIAH 8:1–6; ACTS 13:13–20, 26–41

Expository preaching is that mode of Christian preaching that takes as its central purpose the presentation and application of the text of the Bible. All other issues and concerns are subordinated to the central task of presenting the biblical text. —*R. Albert Mohler*[1]

A VISION OF THE CHURCH must include preaching. The following Scriptures reveal the centrality and importance of proclaiming the Word of God. This is not just a homiletical ideal that should concern pastors. It should concern us all. Indeed, many of our first colleges and universities in America were established in order for future pastors to learn the Scriptures in order to preach—and for people to be educated in order to receive and "inwardly digest" the Word.

The place of the Word of God and the proclamation of the Word of God are central if you are going to achieve a vision of God.

A $50 Bush in a $2 Hole

A man once purchased an expensive plant and proceeded to place it in his garden. He had examined the picture on the tag before purchasing it: a showy rose bush with profuse flowers and healthy green foliage. "The perfect specimen for my flower bed," he thought. He planted it with great anticipation and waited and waited for the blooms. It died. He replaced it. The second plant fared no better; it died as well. He then brought the dead bush to the nursery owner and declared the picture on the tag to be a phony of the highest order. Like a private investigator, he began to inquire as to the placement of the shrub in his yard, the direction of the sun, and so forth. It appeared that he had done everything right. Then the nurseryman said, "Tell me about the hole you dug when you planted it." "Well, it was . . . just a hole," he replied. Removing his glasses in a very paternal way, the seasoned gardener said, "Sir, you have to dig it the right depth, prepare the soil, and treat the soil with fertilizer and mulch." He looked straight at the man and explained, "You can't put a $50 plant in a $2 hole."

$50 Worth of God in a $2 Sermon

We mistakenly expect supernatural transformation to result from humanly devised, earthbound methods.

Your parishioners will want guidance on how to live life, how to build a marriage, how to rear their children, how to deal with sorrow, and how to find silence and solace in their souls in the midst of a construction site world. They expect and may even demand this from the pulpit and from the church. And what are they being fed?

Pastor, be aware of this. While the psychotherapist gets his clients on couches, you get your clients in pews. They do their work one-on-one, and you conduct yours publicly and generally. You want it to be a meaningful experience, so you attend seminars and discover the latest trend in oratorical stylistics and rhetorical wizardry to keep people coming back, to try to help them find God, grow in God, and experience meaning in life.

There are a great many people wanting $50 worth of God out of a $2 sermon; that is, there are many in the pulpit and in the pew looking for the church to grow a supernatural life change from an earthly, finite, human source.

John Stott has remarked, "Preaching is indispensable to Christianity. Without preaching a necessary part of its authenticity is lost."[2] Robert Rayburn, the founder of Covenant Theological Seminary and Covenant College, believed that preaching was so important that it must occupy first place in the studies of seminarians after the study of Christ himself. Rayburn stated, "Christ is the only King of your studies, but homiletics is the queen."[3]

D. James Kennedy, in his retiring moderator's address at the 1989 General Assembly of the Presbyterian Church in America, charged the teaching elders of that Assembly with these words from an old pastor: "Why stoop to be a king . . . when you've been called to preach?"[4]

There can be no argument about the fact that God's plan for building his church involves preaching. "Again the word of the LORD came to me, saying, 'Son of man, speak to the children of your people'" (Ezek. 33:1–2). God tells Ezekiel that he is a guard on the wall, and when he sees the enemy coming, he is to shout the news. In this the people will be saved, if they heed the word.

In Romans, God makes it clear that preaching is primary in his plan for redemption:

How then shall they call on Him in whom they have not believed? And how shall they believe in Him of whom they have not heard? And how shall they hear without a preacher? And how shall they preach unless they are sent? As it is written:

> "How beautiful are the feet of those who preach the gospel of peace,
> Who bring glad tidings of good things!"

But they have not all obeyed the gospel. For Isaiah says, "LORD, who has believed our report?"

So then faith comes by hearing, and hearing by the word of God. (Rom. 10:14–17)

It is right for us to expect and desire a great deal from preaching.

The tag on the plant in Scripture shows that biblical preaching produces healthy, vibrant plants. But it also shows that the source of the message, the hole from which it grows, must be capable of producing such fruit. In other words, there must be God in the preaching to get God in the hearing and God in the living.

Acts 13:13–41 records a portion of the first missionary journey of Paul, Barnabas, and John Mark. John Mark departs, and then Paul takes the lead. The Lord directs them to Antioch in Pisidia (in Asia Minor). There they attend a synagogue service and are invited to speak. It is Paul, though, who preaches. In this passage, you can identify the marks of biblical preaching. If preaching is so important in communicating God's plan for his people, and if you can discern the marks of a biblical message here, then you will have identified a key part of God's blueprint for building his church.

In Acts 13:13–41, every believer may clearly discover, apply, and even expect those marks of biblical preaching.

Biblical Preaching Is Marked by Divine Appointment.

You cannot expect preaching that is anointed by God to produce blessings in the lives of the hearers unless the whole effort is under the divine appointment of almighty God.

In the appointment of a preacher. Paul was led there. The events converged under the hand of God to cause the leader of the synagogue to open up a place for Paul to preach. Paul knew that God had sent him there for such a time as this.

In Acts 13:16, the Scripture says, "Then Paul stood up."

You must be a preacher who stands up. You must be a man whom God prepares, calls, trains, equips, and sends to preach. God did this with Paul, and he has done it with countless others. In any great movement of the church, there has been a man who stood up and said, "God has called me to preach."

Before a man is ordained to the ministry in the Presbyterian Church in America, he declares his call to preach. In fact, he usually is required to declare this to his session, then his presbytery, later to the seminary, again at licensure, then again at ordination. Is God part of that call? Only men whom God has indeed called to preach should assume that task.

Would you go to hear a man preach who approaches the ministry as a career? Would you see a physician or an attorney who practices as a hobby? Of course not; the stakes are too high.

When you are witnessing to someone, you need to understand that God has led you to that time also. It is a divine appointment.

In the appointment of a people. God also appoints the people to whom the preacher brings his message. In Acts 13, God sends Paul and Barnabas to a city in Asia Minor to proclaim the gospel. The Lord makes a synagogue available to them and brings these people together for this occasion.

God moves his people around so that they get what they need to be saved and to grow in the grace and the knowledge of God. You are reading these words today by divine appointment, and this message is for you. There should be expectancy in listening to a sermon, expectancy in reading God's Word, and expectancy in hearing God's Word read.

In all of it, God is sovereign, and in his sovereignty he is accomplishing his perfect will through the appointment of a preacher and a people.

Biblical Preaching Is Marked by a Sense of Mission and Enthusiasm.

Acts 13:16 says that Paul stood up and motioned with his hand. We don't know what this means, except that he was enthused and animated and intentional about what he was going to do. He had a message from God, and he was going to get it out.

Biblical preaching is marked by a sense of mission. Paul had a mission, and the preacher whose life has been changed by God and who has been called by God also has a mission. That sense of mission moves him to go, to look for opportunities to speak, and to address people with enthusiasm.

This sense of mission and the enthusiasm that bubbles up from the soul appear differently in different men. Jonathan Edwards is said to have very carefully read his messages, word for word, from a manuscript. Yet the people heard and many were converted to Christ. Then there was the highly animated—one might even say, theatrical—George White-field, the great evangelist. He expressed that mission and that unction from on high in a very different way.

In other words, if you want supernatural transformation in your life and in the lives of your congregants, you must begin with a sense of mission, and that sense of mission must have changed you first.[5]

Ask your congregation to pray for your sermon preparation and delivery. It's only in this way that you can expect God to use the teaching in your church to build strong disciples of Christ.

Biblical Preaching Is Marked by an Appeal to the Scriptures.

This may be a most obvious point, yet preachers and people alike often miss the blatantly obvious.

The obvious is simply that biblical preaching is marked by an appeal to the Scriptures. It must be grounded in God's Word. This is the force of this passage. Paul did not appeal to anything other than Scripture.

The framers of the Westminster Confession of Faith started, not with the doctrine of God, but with the doctrine of Holy Scripture.[6] Likewise, we do not appeal to the minds and the souls of men with naturalistic proofs, but with the exposition of the infallible and inerrant Word of God.

"Well," you say, "what if they don't believe it." Our answer is that God himself breathed forth this Word, and he breathed air into human beings, and his Spirit can take care of himself. Charles Haddon Spurgeon said that he defended the Scriptures the way he defended a lion—he got out of the way and let it go! Beloved, we cannot expect supernatural results in the lives of our people by teaching anything other than the Word of God.

In many historic churches that are open to visitors, the Bible is often chained to the pulpit to prevent it from being stolen by visiting tourists. This provides an apt picture: you, too, must demand that this book be chained to your sacred desk if anything of eternal value is going to come from your ministry!

Biblical Preaching Is Marked by the Centrality of Christ.

Now, note Paul's sermon itself.

- It is marked by a narrative of God's redemptive work in the Old Testament, in which he chooses Israel, redeems them out of Egypt, gives them the Promised Land, gives them the prophets, saves them, and keeps them.
- Then Paul moves to Jesus Christ and his role as the Promised One of God.

At the center of Paul's preaching is Jesus. He is saying that God's activity in the Old Testament was laying the groundwork for his Anointed One, and that the Anointed One has come and is Jesus. Paul underscores Jesus' life and ministry and declares that we are saved by faith in his life lived for us and in his death that paid for our sins. He is saying that this Jesus has been raised from the dead.

If there is no mention of Jesus Christ and the cross in your sermon, then you are preaching a sub-Christian message. You may have a great ethical message or a moving narrative of some portion of Scripture, but for it to be Christian, it must contain the message of Christ! This truth is powerfully reinforced by Bryan Chapell in his now classic book on the subject, *Christ-Centered Preaching.*[7]

When we preach Jesus Christ, when we support churches that preach Jesus Christ, and when we all—pastor and people—embrace preaching as central to the work of the church, we can expect souls to be saved, lives to be changed, and the world to be transformed. We can expect that children will turn to the Lord, that marriages will be healed, that sorrows will be comforted, that broken hearts will be mended, and that amazing consequences will ensue in our lives when we lift up the King of kings and the Lord of lords! For when Jesus is lifted up, he draws men unto himself,[8] and his Word, which is truth, begins the process—sometimes across generations—of bringing in a new kingdom, his kingdom.

The demand made of Philip is our demand each Sunday: "Sir, we would see Jesus" (John 12:21 KJV).

Biblical Preaching Is Marked by the Message of Man's Sinful Condition.

Paul tells the Jews in this synagogue that the Law of Moses could not save them (Acts 13:39). He says that the only way to be saved is through faith in Jesus. He tells them that they are sinners and have no ability to save themselves through anything they do.

One of the marks of biblical preaching is the announcement of sin. There can be no healing without the diagnosis of the problem, and true preaching does this. David Nicholas used to say, "We cannot give people the good news until they have heard the bad news—the bad news is that they are sinners in need of a Savior."[9]

Many preachers don't like to do this, but it is absolutely necessary. Jesus came to save us from something, and that something is sin and its terrible consequences, including God's eternal punishment.[10]

151

Biblical Preaching Is Marked by the Offer of Forgiveness in Jesus Christ.

Some preachers may not like to preach judgment, but others relish this aspect of preaching and fail to deal with the sixth mark of preaching: the announcement of forgiveness in Jesus Christ.

A faithful church member confided to the pastor of another church that her pastor was constantly scolding the people from the pulpit. The lady exclaimed, "I just want to say, 'Hey, we're here! We came! Help us with our lives, feed us more than God's judgment!'"

Well, Paul does. He offers forgiveness of sins in this passage and says that everyone who believes in Jesus according to the Scriptures will be saved.

God's love and mercy and forgiveness, all personified in his Son, Jesus, must be offered to people. The love of God in Christ can change lives, can heal, can inspire, and can cause love like that to grow in the lives of others.

Biblical Preaching Is Marked by a Warning to Receive Jesus Christ.

Finally, this passage shows the seventh mark of preaching:

- Jesus Christ is offered as Savior to sinners.
- Without Christ, we face punishment, and this must be made clear.

We announce the sinfulness of man, the love of God in Christ, and the new life that is available to all who will confess him, but this must be said with a warning. We know neither the day nor the hour when we will leave this world. So people must be forewarned: Jesus is the only way; they must turn from their sins, from their resistance to his rule in their life, and follow him. In a phrase, repent or perish.

Conclusion

The sermon of Paul in Acts 13 provides incontrovertible marks of a God-centered message. In this we can hope for new life and eternal life. In this we can expect God to do supernatural things in our lives.

The great English Puritan, Richard Baxter, expressed one of the greatest sentiments ever recorded about the work of preaching and its supernatural consequences. The pastor of Kiddeminster wrote a wonderful couplet that I (and thousands upon thousands of other preachers, no doubt) have used before opening the Word: "I preached as never sure to preach again, and as a dying man to dying men."[11]

May every message be preached and received with unction! May our pulpit committees, bishops, district superintendents, and others who have a say in who fills the pulpits of our land focus on these words of Eric Alexander: "Biblical preaching is spiritual in its essence. This is one of the most vital truths about biblical preaching. Let me explain what I mean: the task of true preaching is not essentially intellectual or psychological or rhetorical; it is essentially spiritual."[12]

I would say—and say with the Reformers and the faithful preachers before and after them, as well as the congregation of saints now secure in heaven—that this is the key. A vision of the church in today's world must go beyond rhetoric, style, and personalities. Preaching is essential to the church, whether it is expressed in an Anglican or Baptist, Pentecostal or Presbyterian, Methodist or Mennonite branch of the church. Preaching is the supernatural work of God that brings his "word from another world" into ours. This was the cry of Isaiah in his day, and it is the cry of thirsty souls in ours:

> For as the rain comes down, and the snow from heaven,
> And do not return there,
> But water the earth,
> And make it bring forth and bud,
> That it may give seed to the sower
> And bread to the eater,
> So shall My word be that goes forth from My mouth;
> It shall not return to Me void,
> But it shall accomplish what I please,
> And it shall prosper in the thing for which I sent it.
>   (Isa. 55:10–11)

Questions for Reflection

1. Paul's sermon in Antioch gave a narrative of God's plan of redemption through time. Given the same opportunity, could you present a brief oral history of the church, faith, and the gospel? Consider reviewing this.

2. God has ordained the body of believers around you, even those people whom you have trouble liking or understanding. In the light of this chapter, evaluate your attitude toward difficult people. How can you minister specifically to them?

3. Biblical preaching and teaching are marked by a sense of mission and enthusiasm. How can the church better encourage the pastor and other church leaders in their mission? In what ways have you felt the sense of mission and enthusiasm in your own work, and how has that changed you and your thinking?

4. In what ways do church leaders ensure that the congregation receives biblical preaching and teaching? What is an elder's responsibility to the pastor in holding him accountable? What is the pastor's responsibility to the church laity? Consider how the congregation can be kept vigilant and aware of its role.

5. Examine your heart by writing out a personal testimony that includes your profession of faith. How is the gospel changing you?

Prayer

O eternal and sovereign God, you have called me by divine appointment to serve as an officer in your house. You are hidden from my sight. You are beyond the understanding of my mind. Your thoughts are greater than my thoughts and your ways past finding out. Yet, you have breathed your Spirit into my life, you have formed my mind to seek you, and you have inclined my heart to love you. You have made me restless for the rest of you. You have given me a hunger and a thirst that make me dissatisfied with the joys of earth alone. Lord God, use me in spreading your Word to others. Make me wise to see all thing in light of eternity, brave to face the challenges that such a vision may entail, and joyful in the task of ministry. May all my walk and conversation be such as is appropriate to the gospel of Jesus Christ. In his name I pray. Amen.

12

Living Worship

Longing for the Courts of the Lord

PSALM 84:1–4; JOHN 4:16–26

For Calvin, worship is the sanctifying work of God's Spirit in the hearts of his people. Those who would hear Calvin today must be concerned to discover in our doing of liturgical rites the working of the Holy Spirit. They must aspire above all to glorify God in spirit and in truth. They must pass on through the questions of liturgy to the question of worship.
—*Hughes Oliphant Old*[1]

A BIBLICAL VISION requires a faithful biblical means of realizing that vision. The previous chapter introduced a faithful means of realizing the vision: biblical preaching. In this chapter, we come to the matter of worship. How should God be worshipped? This is the great question of man in the religious world. It remains a question, also, in the church. A woman put this question to Jesus, and you can read his answer in John 4:16–26.

Exactly Where Is God?

A family was on a European vacation. They planned a visit to a great cathedral. The parents told their son that they were going to "the house of God" and that he should be very quiet. They went in and found a seat near the rear of the cathedral. Most of the people there seemed to be tourists like them. The mother whispered to their son, "See the chancel with the decorative sacramental screen. It is absolutely beautiful." Then, in another moment, the father said to the mother, "Did you see those magnificent stained glass windows? Tiffany, I believe." She nodded her head. They went on like this for some time. Then the clergy entered, the choir and the organ piped out a tremendous note, and the service began. It was about then that the little boy appeared quite confused. "Mom, Dad, I see the preacher, I see the choir, I hear the organ . . . but exactly where is God?"

Good question. It is possible to focus on worship and never really come to truly worship God. Perhaps, like the little boy, you have been in churches where there are prayers and singing and nice buildings and lots of music, but you missed the presence of God in your life. You couldn't explain it, but you just knew. Something was missing, and you left wondering where God was in the worship service.

John chapter 4 is about worship. In that passage, a Samaritan woman meets the Lord at a well. In that meeting, Jesus causes her to see her sin. Like any squirming sinner under the conviction of God, she changes the subject. She begins to talk about the "worship wars" of her day. Today, people may argue about traditional versus contemporary worship style or liturgy versus spontaneous form, about instruments or no instruments, and so forth. Actually, much of the controversy over worship today sounds like this woman at the well. And much of it misses the point of the worship that Jesus was talking about.

In fact, Jesus teaches here about vibrant, "spirit and truth" worship, and he even uses the phrase "true worshipers," indicating that there is a true worship and a false worship.

A Puritan named Jeremiah Burroughs wrote a great book entitled *Gospel Worship*,[2] and that is certainly a good name for the worship that Jesus was describing. In the last century, A. W. Tozer wrote about such worship being the "missing jewel" of the evangelical church.[3] A worship service that focuses on the presence of Jesus Christ is most definitely a missing jewel in many of our churches. John Stott refers to worship as "living worship."[4] And what is this? Simply put, living worship is the genuine, heartfelt posture of the soul, which moves beyond questions of mere form to expecting an encounter with the living God.

In John 4, Jesus teaches about living worship. If you are going to be a church that is used by the Lord to achieve supernatural ends, you will have to major in this supernatural means: living worship.

But what defines living worship? We live in an era when we must *face the music*, literally, as in T. David Gordon's *Why Johnny Can't Sing Hymns*.[5] What is at the core of living worship when congregations routinely divide over styles, personalities, instruments, and other practices and attitudes in the matter of worship? One answer is that because worship is important to the life of the church—being the veritable "bucket," as Terry Johnson puts it,[6] that carries theology—it should not be surprising that it is so controversial. Worship should be a priority. It should provoke discussion. We are talking about a response, a rededication to the covenant of grace, in corporate worship.[7] We are talking about the response of creature to Creator. Worship, in all of its expressions, is vital to the community of God's people and our witness in the world. Yet can we identify what living worship truly is? We cannot have a biblical vision of the church today without a biblical theology of worship.

There are five defining features of living worship.

Living Worship Is Not about a Prop, but about a Person.

In John 4:20 we read, "Our fathers worshiped on this mountain, and you Jews say that in Jerusalem is the place where one ought to worship" (John 4:20). Jesus then responds by telling her that a day is coming when true worshippers will not be concerned about locating a mountain, but about locating a person. In other words, living worship is not about a prop, but about a person.

The Samaritan woman seems to be using worship as a diversion in order to avoid the person of Jesus. Arguing about worship is nothing new; it went on in Jesus' day as well as our own. The Samaritans believed that true worship had to take place on Mount Gerizim, where Abraham and Jacob had offered sacrifices. The Jews thought the right place to worship was in Jerusalem. The Samaritans built a temple on Mount Gerizim in 400 B.C. The Jews destroyed it in 128 B.C. Today we hope that a guitarist won't go over and sabotage the organist, but you can see that worship wars are nothing new—and neither is the tactic of arguing about worship rather than worshipping in spirit and in truth.

The writer to the Hebrews wrote of living worship when he said, "But you have come to Mount Zion and to the city of the living God, the heavenly Jerusalem, to an innumerable company of angels" (Heb. 12:22). Living worship is not concerned with mountains or cities. Mount Zion is the place of God wherever God's people are gathered. The city of God is no longer just Jerusalem. It is the place of God's habitation, and he inhabits the praises of his people.

Campbell Morgan declared, "[Worship] is not a question of locality. . . . It is not a question of intellect merely. To worship, men must get down to the deepest thing in their personality, spirit and truth. There must be honesty; there must be reality . . . by tearing off the mask and compelling you to face your own life."[8] This is the gospel principle of worship. Worship is not about a prop, but about the person of Christ.

Worship has principles and elements and expressions. Most of the time, like this woman, we don't talk about the principles and elements; we talk about the expression. A key principle is that our worship must be centered on the person of Jesus, not on some prop or lack thereof. True worship takes place, not on a mountain, not in Jerusalem, but in the hearts of people who confess Jesus as Lord. Jesus didn't let this woman off the hook by getting bogged down in this or that place of worship. He led her to the principle of worship. Jesus will not let you off the hook by talking only about worship expressions. He is always pointing us to the principle of worship: the Lord himself. Jesus Christ is our worship.

Living Worship Is Set in Living History.

You see a second defining aspect of living worship when you read, "You worship what you do not know; we know what we worship, for salvation is of the Jews" (John 4:22).

Here you see that living worship is set in living history. Jesus is teaching that worship takes place in the context of real-life events, which happen under the direction of God.

You cannot worship outside the story of what God is doing in history.

Jesus is telling the woman that true worship is not accepted just because it is motivational or makes the worshipper feel religious or anything of the sort. Jesus is telling her that true worship, a living worship, is set in the history of God's redemption. There must be clear, objective truths tied to worship. God is sovereign. God created us. Man fell into sin and rebellion and misery and was on his way to eternal punishment and separation from God unless something was done. Something was done, and God himself initiated it. God came down and took upon himself flesh and became man in order to save him. Jesus will reveal himself as that God-man.

You cannot worship properly unless your worship is set in that historical-redemptive context. It doesn't matter how good it makes you feel or how motivated you are. Living worship is tied to a living history of God's plan of salvation, centered on Christ.

Bryan Chapell, the chancellor of Covenant Seminary, says that worship must be a week-to-week retelling of the gospel story.[9] This statement is reflective of what the Bible is teaching:

> Remember His covenant always,
> The word which He commanded, for a thousand generations,
> The covenant which He made with Abraham,
> And His oath to Isaac,
> And confirmed it to Jacob for a statute,
> To Israel for an everlasting covenant. (1 Chron. 16:15–17)

Beloved, your worship should be a week-to-week renewal of the covenant in your lives. Each Lord's Day, you should come before the Lord and not leave until you have thanked him and praised him for his salvation wrought in Jesus Christ.

Living Worship Requires a Living Faith.

Note a third defining feature of living worship. In John 4:23–24, Jesus speaks of true worship as being in spirit and truth. This tells us that living worship requires a living faith.

The reference to "spirit" speaks of the fact that our worship is not bound by props and buildings and such. It also shows that only those who are filled with God's Spirit can relate to God in worship, for God is Spirit. To have this spiritual worship, this living worship, you need a living faith.

In 1 Corinthians 2, there is an important passage in this connection: "But the natural man does not receive the things of the Spirit of God, for they are foolishness to him; nor can he know them, because they are spiritually discerned" (1 Cor. 2:14). You cannot worship aright unless the Spirit of God has moved upon you, and you have repented and received Jesus Christ by faith. Only then can you relate to God in worship.

Are you going through the motions of worship? You can sing nicely and know the words and so forth, but is your spirit transformed by Christ? If not, then your worship is not living, but dead. God will not accept worship from a person who is not coming to him in the name of Christ.

Is today the day for you to move from pretentious worship to living worship by yielding your life to Christ?

Living Worship Must Be Based on the Living Word.

In John 4:23, the Lord teaches us to worship, not only in spirit, but also in truth. This leads us to see the fourth feature of a true worship, a living worship. Living worship must be based on the living Word.

Worship should be grounded in the Word of God. There is much talk about worship today—about preferences, about what you like and what your congregation likes, and so forth. But you err if you do not reframe the question. Begin by asking, not what you like, but what God requires. Again, many expressions vary, but the real question is, "How biblical is your worship?" Is it filled with Scripture? God's Word is truth, and this must be the basis for worship.

True worship must also be healing. You should hope that some are saved, that some are encouraged, and that the Spirit of God convicts some before you ever get to preaching the sermon. Why? Because there should be sufficient Scripture in your worship services to bring about healing. God's Word is truth, and the truth will set you free, so you should expect healing to come from every part of our worship services.

Living Worship Leads to a Living Lord.

> The woman said to Him, "I know that Messiah is coming" (who is called Christ). "When He comes, He will tell us all things." Jesus said to her, "I who speak to you am He." (John 4:25–26)

Here, we note the fifth and final feature of living worship: living worship leads to a living Lord.

Jesus' teaching on worship leads to his revelation of himself as the Son of God. Worship that is alive always does that. This revelation, which comes after teaching on worship, leads not only to this woman's salvation, but also to revival and reformation in Sychar. Living worship is all about a living Lord.

When Craig Barnes was pastor at the National Presbyterian Church in Washington, D.C., he held a particular philosophy of ministry concerning their children's worship ministry. Parents were assured that each child would begin to be taught about the worship service, preparing each one to participate with understanding in public worship. At the end of each worship service, the children's director and volunteers invited the children to gather their belongings and sit in the lap of a leader. The leader then whispered to each child, "The Lord loves you." Dr. Barnes said that it was his dream that every child would grow to be a worshipper who heard the whisper of God's love in each service.[10]

That is a good starting place for your vision for worship, not only for the children in your congregation, but also for you. That should be your vision because that is God's idea. Either worship is dry and dead and without the whisper of God's love, or it is a living worship which invites worshippers to come to the Lord and to hear his whisper, "I who speak to you am He."

Oh, may you lead your congregation to know him through your leadership and your worship services! Oh, may you hear his whisper this very day.

Conclusion

In God's Word, nothing is more important than worship, and in the Bible, worship is not a noun. Worship is a verb. In Jesus' teaching, God will not allow you merely to talk about worship or think about worship or study worship or argue about worship styles or props. He is calling you to worship him in spirit and in truth. He is calling you to a living worship, an invitation to be transformed by his grace. From this passage, you have seen that living worship

- is not about a prop, but about a Person,
- is set in living history,
- requires a living faith,
- is based on the living Word, and
- leads to the living Lord.

Where does worship fit into your life?

Evelyn Underhill, a brilliant professor and writer on worship at Oxford, wrote in her book *Worship*: "There is a sense in which we may think of the whole life of the Universe, seen and unseen, conscious and unconscious, as an act of worship, glorifying its Origin, Sustainer, and End."[11]

The Bible says that the very heavens declare the glory of God. Isaiah wrote of the day when the earth and its inhabitants would break out in worship in a paradise regained: "For you shall go out with joy, and be led out with peace; the mountains and the hills shall break forth into singing before you, and all the trees of the field shall clap their hands" (Isa. 55:12). The Shorter Catechism states, "Man's chief end is to glorify God, and to enjoy him forever."

Clearly the worship of God is a priority. But you will never prioritize worship, or, for that matter, truly come to love worship, until your heart is changed, until you experience his love and see that worship is the response of love.

A young woman had to be separated from her mother at a very early age. Her mother had been severely burned, had to go through operation after operation, and was finally placed in a home. The child was placed in the home of her mother's sister, who lived in another part of the country. When she grew up, she learned where her mother was and wanted to visit her. The aunt who had raised her had shown her pictures of her mother as a beautiful young woman, and the girl looked forward to seeing her. She was very nervous as she entered the convalescent home and was led to her mother's room. The nurse tried to warn the girl, but she was so excited that she did not listen. When she walked into the room, her mother was in a wheelchair with her back to the door. When she turned around, the girl screamed. She had never seen such a face—distorted and scarred, barely recognizable as a human face, much less the portrait she had seen as a child. The young woman ran from the room in tears. The nurse followed and found her weeping in a lounge. The nurse told her the story of how as an infant she had been trapped in a fire. Her mother had risked her own life, going through the flames and the smoke to rescue her baby. She got her child to safety, but she was trapped by a fallen piece of the roof. The burns were so terrible that even after numerous surgeries, there was little more to do. The nurse told the girl, "Those wounds are wounds of love for you." The young woman recognized her hard heart, repented, and ran to embrace this woman who had saved her.

This story is a picture of Christ's love for you. You may have a picture of worship in your mind. That picture may be of stained glass windows and Prayer Book language flowing forth with rich choral anthems. Or the picture you are holding may be of a projector screen with cool, contemporary strains pulsating from a praise and worship band. Both of those pictures are expressions of worship, not the principle of worship. The pictures of worship we often carry around with us cannot tell the story of worship. The true image of worship is that of the Man of Sorrows, acquainted with grief, bearing your sins on a cross on a forsaken hill.

Until you come to see Jesus Christ as your Savior, who died for you and who rose again from the dead, and until you believe that the One who loved you to death and back again is here today, you will not worship in spirit and in truth. Until you come to worship and say with Evelyn Underhill, "I come to seek God because I need Him. . . . I come to adore His splendor and fling myself and all that I have at His feet,"[12] you have not truly come to worship.

When hardened hearts are broken by his wounds of love, they are free to worship in spirit and in truth.

This is living worship. Do you attend worship? Do you lead worship? Or do you worship? The answer reveals your vision of the church and your place in that vision. More importantly, it transcends style, region, and contextualization, and focuses worship on the person of Jesus Christ. When he is lifted up, mankind must be falling down in supreme worship and intuitive reverence. For he is God and we are not.

Questions for Reflection

1. Do you wholeheartedly delight in God's Word as you prepare for worship? Can worshippers around you sense your joy? Pray that God would awaken that delight within you and make it evident to others.

2. Consider the various elements of the worship service. How can you better perceive the person of Jesus Christ in these elements? What are you thinking about as you

enter the worship service? What distractions do you need to eliminate?

3. Summarize the gospel in a few sentences. Do you listen for these points in the sermons you hear? How can you relate what you learn to the gospel?

4. Do you worship God out of love or duty? What reasons do you have for worshipping God? What changes might your church need to make in order to clarify the purpose of worship to itself and to visitors?

5. Examine your heart. How can you more fully yield your life to the lordship of Christ? How must the gospel change you?

Prayer

My Father in heaven, please change me day by day, so that I may glorify you and you alone. Help me to be so empty of myself that I may be filled by and controlled by the Holy Spirit in every aspect of my life. Please help me, O Lord, to keep you as my first love and to grow in my love of others for your sake. Keep me grounded in your Word as a lamp for my feet and a light for my path, step by step. May my life truly be a continual living worship of you, so that I may be used by you to effectively lead others in sincere, heartfelt worship of you. May you be wonderfully blessed and glorified by our lives. I pray this in the precious name of your Son, my Savior and Lord, Jesus Christ. Amen.

13

Loving Fellowship

The Church Must Be a Place to Belong

ACTS 28:11–16

The virtuous soul that is alone and without a master
is like a lone burning coal; it will grow colder rather
than hotter. —*John of the Cross*[1]

PAUL HAD SET OUT from Antioch, preaching and planting churches. In Corinth he was rejected, and he declared that
he would never preach to Jews again. Then he learned that
God had saved the ruler of the synagogue. The Lord came
to Paul to tell him not to be afraid, and a new mission began
in his heart. He left Corinth and began a trip to Jerusalem to
preach to his own people. There he was arrested and began
another trip to Rome to appeal to Caesar. In Acts 28:11–16,
Paul sails from Malta on the final leg of the trip to Rome.
As he approaches his destination, fellow believers whom he
doesn't even know come out to him.

As you consider this passage, ask yourself: can you be
a hermit or a monk off in the desert and still enjoy God?
Can we just be private Christians and live out our lives of

discipleship without having to deal with other Christians with all of their problems?

In a biblical vision for ministry, there is another way that God desires you to move forward toward the vision, and that is through loving fellowship.

Left Out

Can you relate to the feelings of being "the new kid" at school with the attendant fears of isolation and loneliness? What about that empty feeling that came from being left out when choosing up sides for a game at recess? Or what about the hollow place inside you that comes from just not having a place to belong? For many people, moving and the process of adjusting and finding a place to belong is a major challenge in life. It is a universal experience of humankind. And it's not just relegated to childhood moves. Everyone needs a place to belong.

Do you remember the television program *Cheers*, with a theme song about a place where everyone knows your name? While bars and clubs may qualify as places to belong, Acts 28:11–16 shows that the theme song of *Cheers* can be replaced with "Blest Be the Tie That Binds." In this part of his Word, God has provided a solution for the pain of humankind by creating the church as a place to belong. It's a place where, even if they do not know your name, everyone knows your condition, your need, and your only salvation. That becomes a vital message in the early twenty-first century, when society is very mobile.

For most of us, relocation brings pain. It brought pain to Abraham, Isaac, and Jacob. It brought pain to the American Pilgrim forefathers who left their home country to found this nation. It brought pain to Paul when he left his career, his home, and his prestige to follow a risen Savior's mandate. There is pain in relocation. But relocation, displacement, moving, and transferring is a part of life now and has always been a part of life.

So you come to this passage and find that the church is the place to belong—a place that, when operating according to plan, becomes a haven of hospitality, a place where others meet you where you are—an "enduring community"[2]—and this is a source of great strength.

Let's examine this text further.

The Church Should Be a Place That Is a Haven of Hospitality.

In Acts 28:11–16, the narrator tells us that the ship left Malta and sailed up to the Italian peninsula. It is interesting to note that they sailed on a ship that had a carved figure on the front of Castor and Pollux, the twin sons of the Greek god Zeus. God's plans for salvation were being unwittingly advanced by idols, which goes to prove that nothing, even profane idolatry, can stop God's plans for worldwide missions. So the ship went from Syracuse—Italy, not New York—to Rhegium and then landed at Puteoli. There Paul and Luke found some Christians. In their next landing, they would be met by Christians, but here we are told that they found brethren, that is, followers of the risen Christ. Upon learning of their common faith, the Christians of Puteoli took them in, and Paul and Luke were given, not just lodging, but a loving place to call home on their journey.

This is the great work of the church. The church is a place to belong to, as it becomes a haven of hospitality. It is a haven because, as with Paul and Luke, the journey can get rough. The journey may include spending time with the hard, salty old pagans. Some of you work with people who are like the idolaters that Paul and Luke sailed with. The journey may include skeptics and those who curse God. It is good that we are there to witness to those who are strangers to the house of God, and we declare that they may come in and find salvation, but we all need a haven of Christian hospitality.

David sang, "Praise the LORD! I will praise the LORD with my whole heart, in the assembly of the upright and in the congregation" (Ps. 111:1). When times were the most difficult, God's people of old, as now, sought haven—sanctuary—with others who had been redeemed.

The church must, now and always, be a place that welcomes us, takes us in, nourishes us, and gives us a home. Don't you want to be that kind of church—that kind of Christian? Such an attitude requires each member to be, in a word, hospitable. This is a Christian who is alert for tired travelers, as Paul was, and is a Christian who seeks to show honor to those who fight the good fight.

Many American communities are fragmented. These torn communities are separated due to various divisions, including ethnic, geographical, and social divisions. Paul alludes to this sort of thing: "Now I plead with you, brethren, by the name of our Lord Jesus Christ, that you all speak the same thing, and that there be no divisions among you, but that you be perfectly joined together in the same mind and in the same judgment" (1 Cor. 1:10).

We live in a world that is filled with division; therefore, we need to be all the more alert to be united in spirit. We need to be all the more intentional about becoming a center of hospitality and warmth for sojourners who are in need of the love of God. That is what the church is to be: a safe haven of hospitality to fellow Christians on their way.[3]

The last part of Acts 28:14 says that after Paul and Luke stayed with these hospitable Christians for several days, they were refreshed. The text reads "so," and that is a big word there: "And so, we went to Rome." In other words, the love and acceptance and attention of the Christians at Puteoli gave Paul and Luke what they needed to send them to where God wanted them to go. In an age like theirs, and in a generation like ours, some who are with us today will be transferred tomorrow. Some will be called away. Some will move. Some are being sent here by God to be ministered to by this body in order that they may serve God somewhere else.

Are you a hospitable Christian? This is undoubtedly an area that requires a renewed commitment because the church is to be God's haven of hospitality in this fast-moving world.

The Church Should Be a Place That Meets Us Where We Are.

In Acts 28:15, Paul and Luke are sent on by the hospitality of local believers, and they continue their journey toward Rome. As they make the journey by land to the capital of the Empire, they journey to Neapolis and then turn northwest on the *Via Appia*—"that oldest, straightest, and most perfectly made of all the Roman roads."[4] There, the Scriptures say, Roman Christians came to meet them. Some came forty-three miles to the Appii Forum—a sort of ancient rest stop. Others came thirty-three miles to the Three Inns rest stop. But the thing to notice is that Luke takes note of it. The kindness of those Christians to welcome Paul and Luke, to meet them where they were, is something that Luke and the Holy Spirit want you to know about.

When the church is being the church of the Scriptures, it consists of the representatives of Jesus, who leave their comfort zones and take long journeys to meet people where they are, at their place in life, at their point of need. The church does that through mission endeavors that are culturally sensitive. This is why there is language training and cultural training. The church meets others where they are on their journey, but it does so in order to bring them into fellowship. The church does that in cross-cultural missions, and it should do the same with our own culture. You must leave your comfort zone and meet fellow believers during the difficult times in their lives. You must reach out to those who are hurting. You must travel the distance and bring hope to those who are in need at a time of loss.

There are times, after a long journey in life, when we need someone to walk with us the rest of the way. Can you recall times in your life when brothers and sisters in Christ left their places and met you at the Appii Forum and the Three Inns of your life? Were you gladdened when you saw them? Journeying takes its toll; thank God for those individuals who are your Lukes, who have come alongside you. Their ministry of presence is powerful, bringing tremendous healing and reminding you that Christ is there with you all the time.

Now you be the Christian who meets others at their place of need, not only in times of sorrow, but also when people are just moving in or going through a change in their life. You must become a person who cares enough to journey out of your comfort zone, to travel where you may never have been before, and extend a welcome in the name of Jesus.

And you never know when you will be the one on the road and need someone to go the distance to meet you.

The Church Should Be a Place That Is a Source of Thanksgiving and Praise.

"When Paul saw them, he thanked God and took courage" (Acts 28:15). Again Luke and the Lord who inspired this text want you to see the power of Christians who go the distance to welcome others on their journey. The effort of those Roman Christians actually caused the worship of God and the advance of the gospel, for Paul responded by thanking God. Paul "thanked God" for those believers who came out to meet them, and he "took courage."

We might say that sincere Christian love is evangelistic. It creates worship and praise; it produces strength to go on. And genuine praise and gratitude to God give courage to believers to press on. Hence, your ministry to another person is not just an act of kindness; it is a ministry of the gospel of Jesus Christ. Jesus said, "For whoever gives you a cup of water to drink in My name, because you belong to Christ, assuredly, I say to you, he will by no means lose his reward" (Mark 9:41).

Some may wonder what their spiritual gift is. But there is not one Christian who can't do what these Roman Christians did in Acts 28:15—go out and meet another person. What resulted in Paul being blessed and God being praised began with someone going out of his way to honor another. That is a gift. Robert Louis Stevenson wrote, "So long as we love, we serve. No man is useless while he is a friend."[5] And that is biblical truth. God is praised and believers are built up when you befriend another person.

Each Sunday morning there are people in your midst who are in need of courage. Some you may know; their situations may be obvious and known to you. You may be God's choice to go and meet them where they are and give them the courage they need to make the journey of faith. Others—well, it may not be as obvious. But make yourself available to the Lord Jesus Christ, to be a cup of cold water for a thirsty soul; he will use you.

The bottom line for a church is this: if people aren't thanking God for the courage, for the blessing they are receiving from that church, then what use is it? God wants his church to be a place that is a source of courage and strength for people who need God's presence and power in their lives.

Conclusion

According to this passage, when the church serves its people as a place to belong, a place that is a haven of hospitality, a place that meets people where they are, then the church gives them courage for their journey.

There is a true story about a businessman who was returning to his home in Rochester, New York, one winter evening. It had been a long, hard, and tiring business trip. He had made his way down the highway and was making a turn toward home, when he saw on the bank of the Genesee River a whole bunch of excited men. He decided to pull over, to take the time to see if he could be of help. He was told that a boy had fallen into the river. They couldn't see him in the dark waters, but they could hear his screaming. The businessman was aghast. "You mean a boy is in there and you are standing here?" The man said no more, but dove into the cold, dark Genesee River. He found the boy, grabbed him in his arms, and struggled with him to the shore. As he wiped the water from the boy's face and brushed back his hair, he was completely shocked. It was his own son. He had plunged in for somebody else's boy, and had saved his own son.[6]

The church of Jesus Christ is a place that takes risks. Believers are people who leave their comfort zone and minister to others, who risk all—imitating Jesus, who gave all.

When the church extends the grace of Jesus Christ, which is received as a free gift from him, to others on their journey, the church is blessed.

There is no club, no fraternity, no association known to humankind like the church, where the only qualification to be a member is a confession of your brokenness, acceptance of God's healing and salvation through his Son Jesus Christ's death and resurrection, and resting in him alone for life and eternal life—where, in dying to ourselves, we live, and in giving away our lives for the sake of others, we find our own life.

This, my friends, is a place of grace, of acceptance, of help along the way, and truly a place to belong.

Questions for Reflection

1. Imagine that an acquaintance is visiting your church. Would he or she be welcomed? Confused? Slighted? Having completed that exercise, what do you need to change about how you yourself relate to guests?

2. Analyze the general unity of your church. Are members well rooted in their communities or do you see a lot of people move and move again? Is the congregation outgoing and friendly, or do members form cliques? Are most activities divided by age, gender, or special interests? Do you have all-church activities and programs outside the Sunday service?

3. How can you be faithful to the gospel while expressing it in terms that appeal to uninformed or uncommitted non-Christians? Do you think your worship services are accessible to young Christians? Do they challenge more mature believers? What might you need to change?

4. How do the members of your church bear one another's burdens? Have you seen the congregation unite in support of a suffering individual? Do members know how to pray for one another? Consider ways in which the church might facilitate greater fellowship.

5. Examine your heart. Do you sincerely desire to know and help even the people who are unlike you? How must the gospel change you?

Prayer

Lord, please make me available to be a loving part of your church, sharing in the concerns of my neighbors, prepared to make clear your good news to overcome sin, making lives brighter and assuring personal salvation through faith in our Lord and Savior Jesus Christ. Amen.

14

Compassionate Outreach

Becoming the Hands and the Heart of God for a World in Need

ACTS 20:33–35

Do you wish to receive mercy? Show mercy to your neighbor. —*John Chrysostom*[1]

PEOPLE ARE WATCHING those in the church to see if there is a difference.

A friend told me about a nanny he and his wife had hired to help with a disabled child. The nanny did not exactly look the part of an au-pair from an exclusive agency in Manhattan. In fact, she looked more like a street artist from Soho! She was tattooed and pierced in places that you might not even imagine. Yet she dined, worked, played, and lived with this Christian family. One day, my friend, sitting at the dinner table, noticed something: the nanny—this young woman with such a different background and faith, or lack thereof—was watching every move his family was making. He had not previously noticed just how intently their nanny had taken everything in. It was as if she was actually examining their lives, their everyday lives, to find something new, something different. He was amazed at how she just watched and listened.

There are many who come and go in our midst who don't know the Lord. They are outside the covenant community called the church. But like that tattooed, pierced nanny, they are watching and listening.

This chapter's lesson comes from Acts 20, where Paul reminds the Ephesian church leaders how he lived among them and how they must live in the world because the world is watching and listening:

> "I have coveted no one's silver or gold or apparel.
>
> "Yes, you yourselves know that these hands have provided for my necessities, and for those who were with me.
>
> "I have shown you in every way, by laboring like this, that you must support the weak. And remember the words of the Lord Jesus, that He said, 'It is more blessed to give than to receive.'" (Acts 20:33–35)

They Must Know That We Care.

There was once a young man who had just graduated from seminary and had taken his first church. He was still excited about a seminary class on Isaiah, so he began to preach a series entitled "Deutero-Isaiah: Hermeneutical Issues and Exegetical Complexities." The first week he had a hundred people. The second week he continued his series and could boast of only seventy-five people. Undaunted, he continued what he thought was a marvelous series and was down to forty people. Within weeks, despite giving them all he knew on the subject, the people left in his congregation could have been counted on two hands. Finally, in exasperation and fearing the worst, he called his old professor. He related his problem. The professor asked him what he was preaching. After hearing the answer, the professor told that student, "Son, they don't care what you know; they want to know that you care."

"They don't care what you know; they want to know that you care" is a good and biblical axiom for every Bible-believing, Christ-centered church today. One of the ways to realize a biblical vision is to engage in compassionate outreach. They must know that you care.

The following words are from the introduction to a book called *Mobilizing for Compassion: Moving People into Ministry*, by Bob Logan and Larry Short:

> The debate gets tiring, especially for those of us who live in the trenches of ministry. On one side are those fervently committed to the task of world evangelism and wanting to see heaven populated with redeemed individuals. On the other side are those whose hearts break for hurting humanity where oozing emotional and physical sores are graphic reminders of the flawed condition of the human soul. My suspicion is that in his divinity, Jesus never struggled with such compartmentalization. Demonstrating compassion and simultaneously seeking the conversion of the heart were irrevocably welded and intertwined in the mind and ministry of the Son of God.[2]

In the early part of the twentieth century, Pearl S. Buck complained that Presbyterian missionaries going to China were emphasizing the gospel too much. She wanted to see missionaries who could meet physical and social needs without giving them the gospel. Later, conservatives reacted against this and went to minister the Word of God without becoming incarnational in their approach.

But where are we today?

I once heard Joni Eareckson Tada tell the unforgettable story of an incident in a fast-growing evangelical church in a conservative denomination. A woman in a wheelchair took her place in an aisle toward the middle of the nave. An usher noticed that the wheelchair was leaving ruts in the plush red carpet that had just been installed. He quietly went to the lady and guided her to the narthex at the rear of the church, where her chair could rest on tile, thus saving the carpet. I always wondered if that person was Joni herself.

That might be an extreme illustration of the problem, but I think our evangelical and conservative churches and Christians in North America need a fresh reawakening to the holistic approach of Jesus Christ to the needs of people.

We must deal with the truth of the gospel and do all we can to get out the message of the sinfulness of man, the holiness of God, and the loving, atoning, and saving work of Jesus Christ on the cross. But we must do so with a caring heart for those around us.

Paul had urged the Ephesian leaders to consider their responsibility to guard the church against coming problems, both savage wolves from without and meddling men from within. But now, after commending them to the grace of God in Christ, the tenderhearted apostle gave them a final charge, the force of which was: "Lead compassionately; become a church of compassion."

In Paul's example and Jesus' entreaty in this passage, we see how God is calling Christians and churches to a ministry of compassion.

How do you move to this ideal presented by the Lord through Paul? In two ways.

Pursue a Life That Is Free of Covetousness.

Paul's example. The apostle Paul ministered in a day when cultic preachers charged for their teaching. Paul surely wanted nothing to do with being placed in their category. So Paul was a perennial tentmaker. Furthermore, when he received gifts, he was scrupulous to pass them on to others. Elsewhere, Paul says that the worker is worthy of his hire (1 Tim. 5:18), and he even goes so far as to say that those who labor in word and doctrine should be given double honor (1 Tim. 5:17). Some believe that this is a reference to pay.

But the passage is really deeper than this. Paul is saying that he has come to the place where he lives free of covetousness. In another place, Paul confesses that God has so worked in his soul that he is happy in whatever state he finds himself (Phil. 4:11).

In his final charge, he tells the Ephesian church leaders to live free of covetousness.

You can have a ministry of compassion, which is the standard here, only if you are free of covetousness, free of the love of money and prestige. Or, to put it another way, compassion begins with freedom from covetousness.

The Scripture's echo. Matthew reports Jesus as saying:

Do not lay up for yourselves treasures on earth, where moth and rust destroy and where thieves break in and steal;

but lay up for yourselves treasures in heaven, where neither moth nor rust destroys and where thieves do not break in and steal.

For where your treasure is, there your heart will be also. (Matt. 6:19–21)

And Paul would write to Timothy, "Godliness with contentment is great gain" (1 Tim. 6:6). Compassion cannot take root in your life until contentment does. In a sense, contentment that brings a freedom from covetousness is simply, as Jesus shows us, trusting in God.

When that happens, tremendous ministries of compassion can take root and grow and flourish to the building up of your treasures in heaven and to the serving of human beings right here and now.

Here is a contented man: Charles Haddon Spurgeon.

Spurgeon's ministry. One of the greatest churchmen of all time was the noted and oft-quoted preacher, Charles Haddon Spurgeon. Although he was known for his unequalled gifts in the pulpit, Spurgeon was, in fact, a man of deep compassion. His ministry of compassion overflowed into the largest city on earth at that time, through the establishment of an orphanage for girls and another for boys, a training college for the poor, a door-to-door literature ministry ("colportage"), ministries to serve the indigent that included providing clothing and food, construction, and community development initiatives. Spurgeon also spoke out for social causes such as the abolition of slavery, workers' rights, and more. There was never a detachment between faith and works. Indeed, Spurgeon's theology became his biography, and his biography became a living legacy of good works that blessed the world in his day—and after. Oh, that we might become in our generation a living, breathing extension of Jesus Christ to the weak and the poor, in word and in deed. Oh, that the world would hear the gospel because they taste it, hold it, wear it, and see it at work in the lives of those who belong to the church of Jesus Christ.[3]

Lord, do it again!

The Christian's challenge. Our challenge today, at least in our materialistic Western society, is to *let go.* You've heard, no doubt, about the monkey who reached his hand through an opening in a tree to get a banana. As he was struggling to get the banana, a leopard spotted him and came after him. The monkey could let go of the banana, remove his hand, and run, or he could hold on to the banana and be unable to get his hand out. This poor monkey was so greedy, so covetous for that temporary pleasure, that he continued to hold on tightly and died with his hand still holding the banana.

That is the undeniable dilemma of the believer living in this age. Is the Lord calling you to *let go*? Let go of trusting only in the things of this world and turn to Christ and his promises. Rest in him alone for eternal life and for every area of life. Stop fretting and begin to live free.

When we do that as individuals and begin to live like that as a people of God, we can move on to be obedient to the Lord and have a ministry of compassion.

Now that is the example of Paul. Consider now the entreaty of Christ.

Practice a Christlike Love for Others.

Paul quotes the Lord Jesus to direct the Ephesian elders on how they must conduct their church.

Christ's entreaty. The saying "It is more blessed to give than to receive" is not recorded in the Gospels. This saying of our Lord was either communicated to Paul by Peter and James or communicated directly to him for our benefit.

It is simple in its command. Blessedness—joy and personal fulfillment—is to be enjoyed by giving, rather than getting. This runs counter to our own fleshly desires, not to mention the base, sinful, primordial urge that undergirds Madison Avenue.

But it is a principle that is often found in the Word of God.

Scripture's echo. Proverbs 19:17 says, "He who has pity on the poor lends to the LORD, and He will pay back what he has given." When you give, remember giving is ultimately an act of worshipping God.

This is not teaching us that poverty is holy in and of itself. Liberation theology, which infiltrated liberal churches in the 1960s and 1970s, seemed to teach this error. It's not that at all. Rather, giving to the weak and the poor, either in goods and money or in time and effort, to improve their lives, is an act of kindness to those who possess the image of God in their person. God uses human kindness as a conductor through which the good news of the soul's salvation flows. This is what James meant when he wrote to wealthy Christians:

> What good is it, my brothers, if someone says he has faith but does not have works? Can that faith save him?
>
> If a brother or sister is poorly clothed and lacking in daily food, and one of you says to them, "Go in peace, be warmed and filled," without giving them the things needed for the body, what good is that? So also faith by itself, if it does not have works, is dead. (James 2:14–17 ESV)

Charles Colson's Reminder

Charles Colson, whose work in founding and leading Prison Fellowship is a model for us all, sought to stir us up to this Christlike approach to others as he recounted the work of the church at its best:

In the nineteenth century, the church organized itself and went to the arenas of need: believers fed the hungry, clothed the poor, and housed the homeless . . . [they] spearheaded most of our nation's significant works of mercy and moral betterment. They founded hospitals, colleges, and schools; they organized welfare assistance and fed the hungry; they campaigned to end abuses ranging from dueling to slavery. Though much of this work has now been taken over by government agencies, Christians provided the original impetus. . . . It was a part of a rich evangelical tradition—and it put into practice the truth that in serving the least of Christ's brethren, we serve Him.[4]

Conclusion

This passage is a final call from Paul to the church at Ephesus: get a heart; strengthen your orthodoxy with compassion.

Jeannie Dunne's Transformation

This story is real. The woman's identity will remain anonymous. We will call her Jeannie Dunne. Jeannie was a registered nurse in Southern California. She was a Christian who knew the Bible and believed it. Her first assignment in a new job was to render service at an AIDS unit. I remember the story that was related about Jeannie like this:

At first it was very difficult. I walked in thinking, *Oh, God, you know this is the last place I want to be.* But as I began working with the terminally ill AIDS and HIV-positive patients, God began to do a funny thing in my heart.

189

For the first time, I began to see the inside person, the true victims of homosexuality and AIDS. God was saying to me very clearly, "You say you love people, so love some of these, society's most rejected." I realized then they are today's lepers. And what was Christ's response to lepers? He courageously and compassionately reached out and accepted them.[5]

God changed Jeannie Dunne's heart. She was already a believer, but her faith took on compassion. She ended up leading her church to reach hundreds of dying young men in Southern California with the compassion of Christ and the good news of Jesus Christ.

Running a Virus Scan on Your Heart

One of the first things that Jeannie had to do, though, was to cleanse her heart. She couldn't begin to have the compassion of Christ until she had rid herself of self.

You have undoubtedly run a virus scan on your computer. Have you ever found that your computer was infected with a virus and thus that every document you produced was infected? In the same way, you need to run a "divine scan" on your life. And what will the scan reveal? Is your life free of covetousness? Are you practicing Christlike love for others?[6] In other words, show the love and grace of Jesus Christ in tangible ways, so that you can teach the gospel of grace. The gospel is believable when the gospel is observable.

And always remember that the world is watching and listening. What do others see? What do others hear?

A biblical vision of the church is not only what we see, but what others must see as well. Let's call a sacred assembly to begin to pray about being the people of God that he calls us to be, *that the world may know . . .*

Questions for Reflection

1. Look for opportunities. What is God calling you and your church to do? Where are the areas of greatest need around you? How can you show the people in your community that you care?

2. In your congregation, whom has God already equipped with compassionate hearts and the gift of mercy? How can you support and equip these people? Do they have a passion that could be extended into a churchwide ministry to others?

3. Find good counsel. Once you have an idea for a new or expanded ministry of mercy, ask trusted brothers and sisters to pray for guidance and any necessary resources. What practical first steps need to be taken?

4. Do you have a sense that the people in your community are watching your church? What sort of face is your church presenting to them? How might you need to change that face?

5. Examine your heart. What do you see there that hinders the compassion you should be showing to others? How must the gospel change you?

Prayer

Lord Jesus Christ, as you wept over Jerusalem, may I weep over my hurting city. As you were deeply moved at the tomb of your friend Lazarus, may I be moved to action over the suffering I see close at hand. Teach me, Holy Spirit, to rejoice with those who rejoice and weep with those who weep. May my heart be broken by the things that break your heart. Beginning today, enable me to take your physical place so that, like Paul, my resources—mind, heart, hands, and feet—will be used to support the weak. May I learn from practical experience that it is, in fact, more blessed to give than to receive. Forgive me for loving things and using people. Turn my values around. May my ministry be one of both word and deed, so that your eternal purposes will be accomplished in and through this, your servant. And may it all be to the praise of your glory. Amen.

15

The Ministry of Prayer

It's All We Have, But It's All We Need

2 KINGS 4:8–37

And Satan trembles when he sees the weakest saint upon his knees. —*William Cowper*[1]

YOU MIGHT BE SURPRISED to learn, in this passage from 2 Kings, that your vision for the future can be located in a story from 800 B.C. in a faraway place called Shunem. In the story of a woman whose desperate need went beyond human capacity to meet that need, you see that in such times, prayer is all you have. But the ministry of prayer, so often overlooked and misunderstood, is all you need.

We Are at War.

As I write, our nation and our world are embroiled in war. And I don't just mean the conflicts in Afghanistan and Libya and the asymmetrical war against radical Jihadist Islamists.

State legislatures, old-line denominations, counties, and corporations are coddling what once was called sin. Opinion polls reveal that our nation is divided down the middle over the moral issues that even twenty years ago would have seemed settled. It seems that whichever direction you look, you see the same thing: wars and rumors of wars over what defines us as a people, over the ethical ground on which we stand.

Meanwhile, the church of Jesus Christ, in all of its various branches, with no single denomination escaping this comment, seems to be fiddling while Rome burns. The national debates, even in many evangelical churches, often seem to have little to do with the fact that a real war is going on—not a war of flesh and blood, as Paul says in Ephesians[2]—but a war against spiritual powers at work in this world. I agree with John Piper: "Until you know that life is war you cannot know what prayer is for."[3]

It is ridiculous to speak of visions and the future without coming to grips with what Piper is talking about. The vision of a church that is equipping the saints for the work of ministry, that is gathering and growing strong disciples of Christ in order to send them out to make other disciples, cannot be realized in a vacuum. You cannot be faithful to a biblical vision without prayer.

Undoubtedly, prayer brought you to your present church. And it will be prayer that allows your church to be used by God as his instrument of grace in this generation. The vision is too divine for any one man or any one group of people to pull off. A divine end requires divine means, and the means that God has supplied for us to move forward is prayer. God works powerfully through prayer to accomplish his will for our lives and our world.

Enter a woman from Shunem. Enter a prophet named Elisha. Enter a sick little boy. The remarkable story in 2 Kings

4:8–37 is not an all-encompassing study of prayer, but it does show the importance of prayer when one is faced with a great undertaking. This passage contains six great lessons on the ministry of prayer.

Lesson 1: The Ministry of Prayer Is the Recognition That We Need a Mediator and an Intercessor (2 Kings 4:8–10).

There was going to come a time in this woman's life when she would need God. She would need a supernatural visitation from the Lord to save her boy. But that supernatural victory, that river of faith, began with a trickle of faith. She believed in this man of God, and she told her husband that they should provide a room for the prophet. They did so, and Elisha stayed there. This woman wanted an intermediary. She wanted an intercessor on her behalf, and she saw Elisha as fitting that role.

None of us would deny that a time will come when we will have need of God. Difficulties will come into our lives. We will face challenges that our intellect and our resources cannot handle. If you say, "I have all that I need to handle any emergency," then ask yourself, "What about your soul? What will happen when your very breath leaves you, and you are cast out into eternity?"

The Shunammite woman believed that Elisha was a man of God. She saw that he could establish a relationship between her and God.

Elisha is a type of the Lord Jesus, who was the man of God, the man from God, the very God-man, and, as Paul refers to him, "the man Christ Jesus" (1 Tim. 2:5 ESV). This woman knew that she wanted the man of God in her home. This was not a lucky rabbit's foot to her. She wanted God in her house. The only mediator between God and man is the man Christ Jesus. Hear the Word of God:

Who is he who condemns? It is Christ who died, and furthermore is also risen, who is even at the right hand of God, who also makes intercession for us. (Rom. 8:34)

Therefore He is also able to save to the uttermost those who come to God through Him, since He always lives to make intercession for them. (Heb. 7:25)

Everything you need begins with inviting Jesus Christ into your life. It would be injurious to this text if you did not see this and respond by welcoming Christ anew into your life.

This is lesson one: recognize that you need a mediator between you and God, one who will intercede on your behalf before the throne of the Almighty.

Lesson 2: The Ministry of Prayer Is Directed to a Savior Who Desires to Give You a Gift (2 Kings 4:11–17).

The Shunammite woman wanted the man of God in her home, so she and her husband prepared a room for him. The man of God then wanted to bless them. He went to their deepest need, a desire for a child, and he interceded and miraculously granted their heart's desire.

This is a picture of our Lord, who desires to give us his gift of grace, his anointing on our lives. His vision is of a church that welcomes hurting people to receive his grace. He wants to see his church gathering and growing strong disciples of Christ who will make other disciples. He wants us to realize this vision.

The Bible says that "the wages of sin is death, but the gift of God is eternal life in Christ Jesus our Lord" (Rom. 6:23). God is the giver of life, and to a fallen race he gave a covenant of grace, whereby he would give his Son for our life and take our sins. And he gives his Holy Spirit to lift crippled sinners out of their depraved condition and carry them to the Son who heals them and gives them the name of son or daughter.

You who are caught in the grips of heartache, won't you receive his free gift of salvation? And if you know the Savior, will you stay away from him? Knowing that he loves to bestow gifts upon his children should make you want to come to him in prayer.

Lesson 3: The Ministry of Prayer Will Be Taken Seriously When We See the Impossible Situation That We Face (2 Kings 4:18–22).

All that could be done for that sun-stricken little boy was done. A distressed father sent the child to the nurturing arms of a wise mother. She held the child. She did all she could for the child, but he died. It was then, at the point of impossibility, humanly speaking, that the woman took the next step. She put that dead child on Elisha's bed and went after the man of God.

This passage is rich in its teaching about resurrection, and it foresees a day when God will raise his own Son, and by faith in him, the bodies of others as well. But it also teaches that when faced with an impossible vision, only a miraculous means will do.

Martin Luther spoke of the place of prayer in the church: "Prayer is a strong wall and a fort for the church; it is a godly Christian's weapon, which no man knoweth nor findeth, but only he who hath the spirit of grace and of prayer."[4]

The Reformation went forth, it is said, on the knees of the saints. It will always advance in prayer. The burden of your vision for the church of our Lord Jesus Christ in our generation—that God would come down and bring revival—

is based upon a conviction that without going to God in prayer, our generation is hopeless. Every sign is pointing to a degenerating society. The increase of ungodliness, the apathy of so many in the church, the wholesale acceptance of sins that the Bible condemns as the sins which will destroy a nation—homosexuality, abortion, disregard of the Sabbath day, profaning the name of almighty God and the Lord Jesus Christ, and so many more—are pointing toward judgment. We have a dying nation on our hands. We have dying people on our hands, and unless there is divine intervention, there will be judgment. This is not a time for a small vision. It is a time for a grand vision, a vision of a third great awakening to come to this nation.

The Shunammite woman knew that the only thing that would solve her problem was God, and she went for the mediator! The vision of this Shunammite woman was for a miracle! She wanted her lad back from the grip of death.

Your vision must not be just for a growing church and some great programs. No, your vision must be for God to shower your life and, through the church, this nation and world, with a fresh demonstration of his Spirit and power and to *save us* from the grip of death and hell and destruction!

So let this portion of God's Word correct your vision and enlarge your understanding of our plight and our condition. Desire a supernatural demonstration from God. We need salvation!

Lesson 4: *The Ministry of Prayer Leads Us to a Willing Lord (2 Kings 4:27).*

"Now when she came to the man of God at the hill, she caught him by the feet, but Gehazi came near to push her away. But the man of God said, 'Let her alone; for her soul is in deep distress, and the LORD has hidden it from me, and has not told me'" (2 Kings 4:27). Gehazi forbade the woman, but she knew that the salvation of her boy rested with that man of God, and nothing was going to stop her. This woman was like the woman in the crowd who had an issue of blood. Even Jesus' predisposed ministry would not stop that woman:

> And suddenly, a woman who had a flow of blood for twelve years came from behind and touched the hem of His garment.
>
> For she said to herself, "If only I may touch His garment, I shall be made well."
>
> But Jesus turned around, and when He saw her He said, "Be of good cheer, daughter; your faith has made you well." And the woman was made well from that hour. (Matt. 9:20–22)

Gehazi, on the other hand, is like the disciples in the New Testament who thought the honor of God limited his desire to reach out to people in need. They thought, like Gehazi, that they were doing their Lord a favor by keeping mothers and their infants from the Master. But God delights in answering prayer. Elisha said, "Let her alone!" God welcomes you with your need in this moment.

When your burdens, your vision, your need of healing, your need of salvation, or your need for wisdom drives you to God in prayer, you have a God who is willing to demonstrate his glory through answered prayers.

It has been said, "Prayer is not overcoming God's reluctance; it is laying hold of his highest willingness." And so we go to God and cry, "Unless you come and visit us, Lord, we have no hope." But the very character of God, who sent his son, demonstrates that you are praying to a God who answers prayer and who delights in blessing his people. Thus, be most confident and excited about the future, no matter what the news of the day may be. Almighty God is still on his throne, and you can cry out to him with confidence for the salvation of your loved ones. You can pray for revival with confidence. You can hope for the best, wish for the best, and expect the best from the God who says, "For all the promises of God in Him are Yes, and in Him Amen, to the glory of God through us" (2 Cor. 1:20).

Lesson 5: The Ministry of Prayer Is Not about a Religious Ritual, but about the Power of God on His Anointed One (2 Kings 4:31–35).

This lesson comes after examining two elements in this part of the story:

- Gehazi's efforts in raising the child from death were futile (2 Kings 4:31).
- Elisha alone was anointed for such a death-defying ministry (2 Kings 4:34–35).

Gehazi has no power, for he does not have the anointing of God. Indeed, in 2 Kings 5:20–27 he is revealed to be a greedy man wanting only personal gain. He is a hireling in the service of his own greedy ends, not God's will, and he will be judged.

As soon as Gehazi left, the woman grabbed the man of God and said, "I'm not leaving you." She was laying hold of God and his promises. Gehazi would not do; superficial ritual would not do. She knew that only one thing would heal her boy, and that was the prophet.

Mere religious ritual is judged as impotent in the face of supernatural needs. Only one thing can meet the vision that

God gives you to see souls saved and lives built up. Only one thing can meet your great need, and that is God. Only Christ, raised from the dead by God the Father, can transform enemies of God into sons and daughters of God or repair broken dreams or bring life from death.

Now, this is what the divinely inspired author of Psalm 46 knew when he wrote:

> God is our refuge and strength,
> A very present help in trouble.
> Therefore we will not fear,
> Even though the earth be removed,
> And though the mountains be carried into the midst of
>   the sea;
> Though its waters roar and be troubled,
> Though the mountains shake with its swelling. *Selah*
>   (Ps. 46:1–3)

Each of us in the church is aware of families in trouble. The stories of heartache and sorrow that come to my own office, as a minister, do not lessen over the years, but seem to surge. We seem to witness earthquakes of divorce, mountains of hopes and dreams slipping into the heart of a furious sea. You sometimes hear the glaring "music" of our age and wonder whether it is a sound track of a whole generation slipping into hell.

But, my dear reader, there is a God whom the psalmist calls "our refuge" and "our strength." There is a God who came down to be born into a hellish storm when Satan used a madman named Herod to try to kill the Son of God. This God, who is called the Holy One, faced the mountains of hate crashing upon his soul as he writhed in agony on a Roman cross. This God, who is without sin, became sin so that we who are sinners could be called the holy ones of God. This God faced the storms and is still standing. And he invites you to bring your children's problems to him, to bring your marital problems to him, to bring your storms and your mountains to him, to lay your dying dream down and forget Gehazi-like solutions and call upon the One who is your only refuge and your only strength.

Lesson 6: The Ministry of Prayer Transforms the One Who Prays (2 Kings 4:36–37).

At the end of the story, the child is healed. Miraculously, the child is raised up. All of this is pointing to the resurrection power of Jesus. But this woman was transformed also. Her heartache was lifted, and she knew more of the power of God after this episode than before. Do you believe that this one who was raised from the dead did not also serve the Lord?

God, in answered prayer, changes things and changes people and even changes generations.

In Psalm 46:8, the psalmist writes, "Come, behold the works of the LORD."

The testimonies of God's people are a great force for revival. Pray that your church is now and always will be a praying church, and that as God surely answers prayers, raises dying dreams, and resurrects families and people who have lost hope, the testimonies of grace will be told. And people in your community will gladly proclaim, "Come, behold the works of the Lord."

Conclusion: Finding Your Way with a Slide Rule

Who can ever forget those days, if you were alive in that time? Or, through the power of cinema, who is not familiar with the famous line, uttered in outer space, by actor Tom Hanks?

"Houston, we have a problem," Commander Lovell said as his Apollo 13 spacecraft tumbled out of control over 200,000 miles from Earth. Those infamous words were the start of an odyssey that caught the world's attention. What almost became the worst tragedy in NASA's history became NASA's greatest achievement. In many ways, returning the astronauts back to earth alive was more of a technological challenge than landing a man on the moon.

The problem was a ruptured oxygen tank which severely crippled the spacecraft. There was not enough oxygen, power, electricity, or heat to get them back alive. It seemed totally hopeless. What made matters worse was that several times while ground control was struggling to resolve one problem, another problem would raise its ugly head. Sometimes a life-threatening problem would have to be resolved in minutes. I found it interesting when dozens of engineers pulled out their slide rules and made frantic calculations to plot new solutions. The computers and calculators we take for granted today were not available then. Calculations we can now do in seconds, took hours and even days back then.[5]

Like Apollo 13 and the Shunammite woman, we, too, have a great problem before us. Our nation is in need of revival. And so it is time for Christians to go back to the old standard. When we are faced with an impossible situation, we need to go back to the basics. But we had better be trained in the basics. We had better know what is going to get us home. It is not our ingenuity; it is prayer.

How do you land this impossible dream, this vision of a church, of transforming grace, of lives being saved? How do you continue and build it for the future? Not through fancy programs or novel ideas from the marketing department, but through prayer.

And that requires Christians to do a few things.

- Commit to the ministry of prayer.

  Admit that unless you pray, you're sunk. Make prayer the priority in your life as well as the priority of the church.

- Pray the Scriptures.

  Go to God with his very Word and plead for this generation, this world, this nation, this race of mankind, and cling to the cross in your prayers. There alone is our hope—there, where the Son of God hung, being crucified by those he had created, and looking down, with a love that we cannot begin to understand, said, "Father, forgive them, for they know not what they do."

A Vision That Is on Its Way

On the cross we see pure love—not a reactive love, but a creative divine love—a love that initiates, that goes beyond what we could ever imagine, that gives more, extends farther, goes deeper, and climbs higher than any love we could imagine. This is our hope. To come to God in prayer, then, is to climb to the peak of human experience in this life and to touch the throne of grace. And to have gone there, fellow sojourner, is to have a confidence in the midst of the wars of this world, a confidence that says the kingdom of Jesus Christ is here and yet is still coming. The kingdoms of this world are already becoming the kingdom of our God and of his Christ. The knowledge of God is spreading as the waters cover the sea. Thousands of human beings are being delivered each day from the kingdom of darkness and brought into the kingdom of God. Millions of those who have gone before are surely prepared to hear the war cry of King Jesus, as his Father says, "It is time!" The skies will be rent in two, and the trumpet of God will blast through the universe. Those who have died in Christ will rise, and then we who are left will be caught up with them to be with Jesus in a new heaven and a new earth—with a new body and a glorified soul—forever and ever. Then will Eden be restored. Then will mankind be returned to the place of no night and no tears and no sea to separate us. Then will we sing with the joy of an innocent child, and recall the glories of Christ's salvation, even as we, surely, carry on with a new good work in that new garden. There will we gather at the river. There will we sing with hearts filled with redemptive joy.

Abraham and Moses, Peter and Paul, Athanasius and Augustine, Calvin and Wesley, Edwards and Asbury, your mother and my father, cry out as one: "Call for a sacred assembly!" Then, perhaps, the angels and archangels, and the prophets, martyrs, and saints of all seasons may cry. But their call for a sacred assembly will not be a call to repent in sackcloth and ashes, but to join with the lamb and the lion, with all races of men, and all generations of the earth, to give worship and exaltation to the Lord Jesus Christ. Then we will know what we dream of in part now: that the church is the ransomed joy of her Lord, and she has endured, and there she has gathered, as we used to say in our creed, "world without end." Perhaps, on that day, in eternity future, we will also sing with victorious voices what we sing with hopeful hearts today: "Till with the vision glorious her longing eyes are blessed, and the great church victorious shall be the church at rest."[6] No vision less than this one for the church today is worthy of the church and her glorious Lord, our Savior and God, Jesus Christ.

Questions for Reflection

1. Consider what stops you from trusting that God gives good gifts to those who ask him. How should you live to show others that you really believe that God desires to give good gifts to you, his child?

2. Reflect on your church's prayer life. Do the members of your church pray together? Do they consider these times important? What do they pray about? Do you celebrate answers to prayer? Is the power of prayer mentioned in sermons?

3. How often do you consider Jesus' role as Mediator? Is this role ever impressed on the congregation? Jesus' mediation gives you many reasons to be hopeful; list a few.

4. During what times in your life have you prayed deeply out of deep alarm? How can you better remember that the bride of Christ is at war? How can your church better emphasize the urgency of prayer?

5. Examine your heart. Why is it hard for you to trust that God will manifest his strength on your behalf? How must the gospel change you?

Prayer

God, my Father, thank you for giving your only Son to suffer the penalty for my sin. Thank you for raising Jesus from the dead and seating him at your right hand. I also thank you that Jesus intercedes with you on my behalf. Please help me to take you at your Word. Please help me constantly to come to you in prayer and find in you the peace, refuge, and confidence that you promise. Please show yourself strong on my behalf and on behalf of our group of believers. Please help me and our church to be faithful and obedient to you and your commands. Help us to live in such a way that others will see your hand on us. Help us to live so that you get the credit, the honor, and the glory. I pray this in Jesus' name. Amen.

APPENDIX A

The Implementation of a Vision and Ministry Plan for a Local Church

THERE IS MORE to implementing a vision and ministry plan for a local church than just preaching sermons, though the preaching of the Word is not only indispensable in the task, but may even be most important. Yet the work of the pastorate calls for the gospel minister and local church leaders to wrestle with finding the burden of God in his Word, with bringing out the core values of the Bible, and with setting the vision, mission, and philosophy of ministry in the context of the church's locality. This having been said, allow me to share three critical aspects of implementing a vision and ministry plan. In fact, I would say that these must be in place in order for the vision and ministry plan to move from paper to reality.

A Burning Man

Benjamin Franklin is said to have always made it a practice to go hear the great evangelical George Whitefield whenever he was nearby. When asked why he never missed going to a Whitefield preaching session, the redoubtable

Franklin is reported to have said, "Because I have never seen a man burn alive."

It is certainly true that vision begins in the heart of one man. The work of developing and implementing a vision and ministry plan for the local church is conceived in the very life of the pastor. It must be this way. A contrived plan, brought about just by reading this or some other book, cannot yield the eternal fruit that you surely desire. The vision must begin as a work of the Spirit in the pastor's life. I am not saying that this excludes the local elders or deacons, but I am saying that Christ gave pastors to equip the saints. If he is not sure of a burden, convicted by core values, strengthened in his own eyes by a glorious vision from God's Word, or shaped in his understanding of how to reach that vision, then no one else will get it. This is the undeniable, mandatory responsibility of the man of God called to pastor a flock of Christ's sheep. Hurry to the secret place! Hurry to your knees in prayer! Hurry to the Word and spend time there until you are burdened, until you are convinced and convicted of Christ's truth in your own heart. Then, and only then, should such a vision and ministry plan be undertaken.

Running Through the Thistles

There is an old story about how to get across a field of thistles. One way, it is said, is just to start running as fast as you can! You will get to the other side of the field quicker that way. It will be painful, and on the other side you will spend a great deal of time picking out thorns and dealing with the lingering pain, but it is quick. But there is another way—a slower, but better way. One may visually plot a path through the thistle field and then carefully, slowly, deliberately, cautiously, but resolutely begin the journey.

Going into an existing church is like entering a field of thorns. Pastors and church leaders who fail to survey the field, who proceed without plotting a path, and who choose the harder but quicker option of running through the thistles, are in for a lot of pain. And they are in for a slowdown at the other end of the field. In fact, the journey may even stop right there.

All of this is to say that the burning in one's heart for ministry must lead to careful planning for implantation. We shepherd the flock of Christ. We are to be gentle, discerning, and careful about Christ's sheep, as well as wise in our outreach to lost sheep out in the world.

Listen, Learn, and Love

Here are three good steps to take.

Listen

Pastors and church leaders surely are not to be a reed blowing in the wind or like an unprincipled politician taking positions only after having been advised about the latest opinion poll. Yet there is wisdom in taking time to listen to the questions, to hear the bleating of the sheep—and possibly even to hear the cries for help. It is, indeed, out of this step that a burden arises.

Learn

One important lesson I have learned in my transition into a great, historic congregation is that I have many lessons to learn. Pastors, particularly those entering new fields of service, must listen to the stories of God's grace, as well as the stories of pain. And in listening you begin to learn. You must also learn what is important and why. We often joke about learning where the land mines are located. There is truth in that. It is also wise to understand the heartbeat of a congregation, to study their history in order to discover the work of God that has gone on before you. C. S. Lewis would speak of "chronological arrogance." There can be chronological arrogance in the minister who comes into a church believing that nothing good ever happened there until the congregation had the good sense to call him! How ungodly— yet how common, if pastors would admit it. Ministers must give their lives away for the sake of the elect, give their lives away to a cause that is greater than themselves, and love the flock entrusted to them by the Chief Shepherd. Praise God for your predecessors and honor them. Show honor to the saints who have been around longer than you. It is true that you will have a word to share with them. But they have something to offer you.

Love

The sheep must know that Christ is loving them through your ministry. A prophet who comes in browbeating the saints who faithfully show up will create a storm, but not cultivate a flock. An academic who retreats to his study will not win the hearts of his people. When he seeks to share a vision, they will reject it (as godly and perhaps even as biblical as it may be) because it didn't come from the shepherd's heart. Likewise, a man who has only preached the vision without loving the sheep may cast a vision, but he will never capture hearts.

I was reminded recently of the differences between the struggling, wrestling faith of Jacob and the releasing, trusting faith of Ruth. Jacob fought and plotted and wrestled his life for the dream. It was hard. It created constant strain on himself and others. Ruth, however, simply followed. Her faith led her to be released, with all the freedom that such faith brings, into the strong, loving hands of a sovereign God. I was reminded of the differences between Jacob's faith and Ruth's faith as I was reflecting on my faith. I confess that the hot blood of Jacob surges through my veins. As I have begun pastoral projects, I have approached them like taking a beachhead for God. And the wrestling and struggling over the establishment of a vision lasted all through the night. I was left tired and hurt. Others, too, felt the pain of my struggle, most notably and regrettably my wife. But there is another way, and when I have been most in step with the Spirit, I have experienced the freedom of Ruth's faith. I have been able to say, truthfully, "Let the beauty of the Lord be upon me, and *establish the work of my hands for me, yes, you establish the work of my hands*" (from Ps. 90:17—the verse I have used to dedicate my ministry goals to Jesus Christ in both church plants and the pastorate).

Listen. Learn. Love. Begin your ministry well. And you will know the redeeming power of Christ at your side. You will sense his hand upon you. You will witness his power at work through you. And you will be free.

I am convinced that a minister of the gospel must *become* a pastor. He cannot simply be called the pastor. The time for that transformation to occur is often, but not always, during his entrance phase. That time has been called the honeymoon. If there is such a thing, then I would suggest that two things have to happen during the so-called honeymoon of a pastor and people. In large part, these things are within the purview of the work of the Holy Spirit. First, sometime, somehow, the congregation must be able to say, "Pastor really cares." That can happen because of your presence during a crisis in a family or your loving leadership exhibited in a tense board meeting or in some other way. There will always be those who don't sense this, but most of the congregation must know that you love them. Second, there must come a time when the people are able to say, "There is a future." Again, I must emphasize that the pastor and church leaders cannot manipulate this. They can and must pray for it to happen, but it can only happen by the hand of God. There may be such a moment at a Christmas Eve service that is well attended, or at a missions conference where the goal is met, or it may have nothing to do with larger offerings or bigger attendance figures. This serendipitous moment may occur during a sermon or at a church picnic. But something must happen where the people begin to see, not only that you love them, but also that you are with them for the future.

After you have listened for the stories of God's grace among your sheep, and have learned what God is doing or perhaps even what the devil is up to or how Christ is walking among them—then and only then, through prayerful reflection on these things, should you call for the leaders to say, "I am burdened for God's glory in our midst. I want us to lead this flock. And this is the way we must go."

The Vision and Ministry Statement

FIRST PRESBYTERIAN CHURCH OF CHATTANOOGA, TENNESSEE

Let Your work appear to Your servants,
And Your glory to their children.
And let the beauty of the LORD our God be upon us,
And establish the work of our hands for us;
Yes, establish the work of our hands. (Ps. 90:16–17)

Preamble

This Vision Statement was prepared by the senior pastor as a major part of his responsibility to cast a biblical vision for our ministry together at First Presbyterian Church of Chattanooga. The Vision Statement got started with a burden on the heart of one man. By the end, it expressed, hopefully, the burdens and dreams of many coming to meet in a pastor's heart.

The Vision Statement was formulated through many hours of praying, breaking bread, laughing, and, on several occasions, crying, with the saints (and not a few seekers) of First Presbyterian Church of Chattanooga. This part of the vision planning was called "Listening,

Learning, and Loving." It was an intentional and, hopefully, "organic" experience of pastor and people growing together. There were formal ways in which the Vision Statement came together, of course. There were meetings with the Ad Hoc Committee on Committees and Reorganization. There were meetings with elders, deacons, and the Women in the Church (WIC) to hear their hopes and dreams. There were meetings with staff and committees and Sunday school classes, and with both longtime members and new members. But in the end, it was one man before the Lord, seeking to merge many dreams into one dream.

I want to honor the following ruling elders who lived out their calling so well in guiding, supporting, challenging, and always encouraging me:

Mr. Pete Austin III, Mr. Scott Brown, Jr., and Mr. Robert Venable, Sr.

Honoring the Past

> Remember those who rule over you, who have spoken the word of God to you, whose faith follow, considering the outcome of their conduct. (Heb. 13:7)

Our vision begins by acknowledging and honoring the vision that has gone before and building on it, and never departing from it. First Presbyterian Church (FPCC) has been and will remain a church committed to historic, Bible-believing Presbyterianism, a strong Sunday school, world missions, home missions, and being a loving, caring fellowship for all who will come and worship Jesus Christ with us.

Thus, we are building on that vision with this new pastorate.

The Burden for Vision

> Oh, that You would rend the heavens!
> That You would come down!
> That the mountains might shake at Your presence.
> (Isa. 64:1)

Our vision begins with a burden for God's glory in our generation. We long to see people released from the bondage to sin and shame and an eternity separated from God, from never realizing their joy as created beings of God, and thus we dream of being a church where people will be fulfilled as they come to glorify and enjoy God through repentance and faith in Jesus Christ. We long to see souls safe in the arms of Jesus on the day when he comes again.

The Core Values for Vision

> Oh, how I love Your law!
> It is my meditation all the day. (Ps. 119:97)

Our vision is informed and guided by these core values:

- A passion for God's Word (Scripture)—2 Timothy 3:16–17,
- A heart for God's world (evangelism)—Matthew 28:16–20,
- A commitment to God's grace (the Reformed faith)— Ephesians 2:8–9, and
- A priority on becoming an equipping church— Ephesians 4:11–16.

Thus, the staff is committed, not to do ministry, but *to equip disciples to do ministry* (according to the Word of God, for the sake of Christ in evangelizing the world, faithful to the doctrines of grace illuminated during the Reformation).

The Vision Is about Who We Must Become.

> Now to Him who is able to do exceedingly abundantly above all that we ask or think, according to the power that works in us, to Him be glory in the church by Christ Jesus to all generations, forever and ever. Amen. (Eph. 3:20–21)

FPCC seeks to be an equipping ministry of God's grace, transforming the lives of people in Chattanooga, our nation, and the world as we proclaim Jesus Christ as Lord of all.

In using the words "FPCC seeks," we want to begin by saying that who we are, what we will become, and where we are going as a church, are surrendered to the sovereign will of the Almighty. We seek to present our vision with humility, completely dependent upon the Lord.

In speaking of "an equipping ministry," this vision seeks to show that we want to be an equipping church— a church where people can be welcomed into the fold of God's family and find their place in his body as healthy disciples.

In using the words "God's grace," this vision seeks to focus on the doctrine of grace as the core doctrine that saves us, keeps us, and brings us into relationship with God and each other.

As we speak of a church that is "transforming the lives of people in Chattanooga, our nation, and the world," we mean to say that we hold the gospel to be victorious and that Christ's kingdom is marching successfully through history toward the day of his return. We are confident in the gospel and expect that, as we faithfully call people to repentance and faith in Jesus Christ, many will come, and as they come, the Holy Spirit will bless his Word and transform their lives. The scope of our work is set forth by the Scriptures, Old and New Testaments, and especially the Great Commission (Matthew 28:16–20), which calls us to a worldwide ministry.

When we speak of an intention to "proclaim Jesus Christ as Lord of all," we mean to say that our vision is to lift up Christ as the first and only source of salvation for fallen people and as the Lord of every area of life. Thus, this speaks to our world-and-life view of Christ's rightful claim over every aspect of life.

The Mission Is How We Will Get There.

> But you shall receive power when the Holy Spirit has come upon you; and you shall be witnesses to Me in Jerusalem, and in all Judea and Samaria, and to the end of the earth. (Acts 1:8)

Our mission is to be gathering and growing strong disciples of Jesus Christ to be sent forth to make disciples.

By "gathering and growing," we mean to say that we are intentional about going out to seek the lost, the broken, and those in need of a church home. By "growing," we mean to grow in the grace and knowledge of Jesus Christ. A strong disciple is one who is exercising the means of Christian growth (Word, sacrament, and prayer), especially in the areas of Bible study, worship (personal, family, and common worship), fellowship, prayer, and witnessing. The goal is not just to gather and grow strong disciples, but in obedience to the Lord to equip them to be sent forth to make other disciples.

The Philosophy of Ministry Focuses on Those Matters of Ministry Which We Prioritize to Accomplish the Mission to Achieve the Vision.

> But God forbid that I should glory except in the cross of our Lord Jesus Christ, by whom the world has been crucified to me, and I to the world. (Gal. 6:14)

Our philosophy of ministry is to accomplish this mission and prayerfully realize this vision by:

- Expository Bible teaching and preaching,
- Living worship,
- Loving fellowship,
- Compassionate outreach, and
- The ministry of prayer.

By "expository Bible teaching and preaching," we mean gospel proclamation and instruction that is grounded in strong exegesis of the Word of God, and in which the truth of God is applied to contemporary living with love and grace.

By "living worship," we mean public services of worship based upon principles and elements gleaned from Scripture, with an expression of worship that is reverent and humble. The service uses psalms, hymns, and spiritual songs that are as diverse as the contributions across the centuries, yet conditioned by the principles of worship drawn from Scripture. Living worship is filled with Scripture, participatory, expectant, seeking to engage heart and mind, done with excellence for Christ, emphasizing God's transcendence and immanence, in spirit and in truth, reverent, connected with the best traditions of worship, yet alive with a prayer for the power of the Holy Spirit to do his great work in our midst.

"Loving fellowship" speaks of our common life in the Lord Jesus Christ. We are in community with God through Christ and thus in community with each other. While recognizing the diversity of gifts, backgrounds, ideas, and experiences, we glory in our unity in Jesus Christ and seek to encourage each other in him.

By "compassionate outreach," we mean to say that we must be intentional about reaching the poor, the downtrodden, and the lost in tangible ways as we reflect God's love for them.

By "the ministry of prayer," we mean to say that the burden is lifted only through a vision grounded in prayer. Only God can cause this vision to be realized. Moreover, we believe that in prayer, we who would be used of God are necessarily transformed.

A Concise Statement

FPCC has a burden to see God's glory in our generation, which alone can bring the revival of true faith and the reformation of society that we so desperately need. FPCC is built on the core values of a passion for God's Word (Scripture), a heart for God's world (evangelism), a commitment to God's grace (the Reformed faith), and a priority to be an equipping church.

FPCC is a ministry of God's grace, transforming lives in Chattanooga, North America, and the world as we gather and grow strong disciples of Jesus Christ to be sent forth to make other disciples. To achieve our vision, we will emphasize expository Bible preaching and teaching, living worship, loving fellowship, compassionate outreach, and the ministry of prayer.

A Brief Vision Statement

"A ministry of God's grace, transforming lives through the gospel of Jesus Christ."

A Brief Mission Statement

"Gathering and growing strong disciples of Jesus Christ."

Strategic Pastoral Priorities

For I know the thoughts that I think toward you, says the LORD, thoughts of peace and not of evil, to give you a future and a hope. (Jer. 29:11)

Some of my initial pastoral goals related to this plan include:

1. **Kingdom Prayer**—Inaugurating a Kingdom Prayer Campaign to enlist a growing number of people at FPCC to lead in praying for revival and reformation and to pray that this focus on prayer spread to other churches in our city. Being a "sending church"—an Antioch for the twenty-first century (Acts 13:1–3)—requires becoming a congregation focused on kingdom prayer.

2. **Leadership Development**—Reorganizing our leadership to emphasize elders as shepherds and deacons as ministers of compassion as well as service, and reorganizing our committee structures to follow our Vision and Mission Plan for FPCC.

3. **Community Caring**—Organizing congregational care groups, where each group has elders, deacons,

Women in the Church representative(s), and one of our ordained ministers.

4. **Outreach and Assimilation Plan**—Developing a systems-design approach to outreach and assimilation, which will build a pathway for visitors moving from a first visit to church (from the time they arrive in the parking lot) to a day when they are leading others to Christ and bringing them to church.

5. **Evangelism Training**—Beginning an evangelism-equipping ministry (EE) to afford the opportunity for every member of our church to be trained in personal witnessing, in order to present a clear, cogent presentation of the gospel.

6. **Evangelism in the Community**—Beginning an evangelistic outreach to skeptics via evangelistic small groups and world-and-life view conferences for the community.

7. **Campus Outreach**—Bringing the Reformed University Ministry campus minister into our staff and ministry environment, and beginning to work with his staff to create a growing strategic partnership between UTC and FPCC.

8. **Church Planting**—Creating a Church-Planting Apprenticeship Program to send forth assessed, trained, and kingdom-visionary church planters throughout North America. This program will be assisted by Mission to North America as we strategically partner to reach North America with new, strong Reformed and evangelical churches.

9. **Compassionate Outreach**—Organizing pastoral care felt-need small groups for grieving over loss and divorce recovery (à la Stephen Ministries).

10. **Children and Singles Ministries**—Staffing for greater impact (gathering, growing, sending) in children's ministries and singles ministry.

11. **Comprehensive Ministry of Music**—Introducing a comprehensive music ministry based on "excellence in all things and all things for Christ" and involving children's choirs, youth choirs, praise and worship ensembles, orchestra, and adult choirs.

12. **Enhancing Worship**—Having implemented new worship services which (in the morning) emphasize God's transcendence through the historic Reformed liturgy, and (in the evening) emphasize God's immanence through praise and worship stylistics, we now begin to further enhance these services by integrating both styles, with excellence and careful timing.

13. **Facility Planning**—Appointing a Facility Planning Commission of the congregation to work with our architectural firm to develop a facility Master Plan to be presented to the Congregation.

To meet that vision, our Leadership and Staffing Plan is emerging to look like this:

Elected or Called Leadership of FPCC

Jesus said to him, "Feed My sheep." (John 21:17)

Session

- Primary oversight for all programs and ministries of FPCC according to the PCA Book of Church Order
- Shepherds of the congregational care groups of FPCC
- Assuming all prerogatives granted by the PCA Book of Church Order

Diaconate

- Carrying out duties to assist the Session and senior pastor according to the Book of Church Order
- Delegated oversight of finances and property of FPCC
- Oversight for ministries of compassion to membership
- Assisting to facilitate the worship services of FPCC (ushering, parking lots, visitor assistance, security)

Senior Pastor

- Spiritual leader and vision casting for FPCC
- Primary pastor-teacher and worship leader for FPCC
- Moderator of the Session
- Staff leader
- Ex officio member of the diaconate, and on all committees and subcommittees of FPCC
- Chairman of the Financial Oversight Committee

Pastoral Staff of FPCC: Members of the Pastor's Advisory Team

Subordinate ministerial or assistant director positions are listed beneath the department heads **in bold**.

And He Himself gave some to be apostles, some prophets, some evangelists, and some pastors and teachers, for the equipping of the saints for the work of ministry, for the edifying of the body of Christ, till we all come to the unity of the faith and the knowledge of the Son of God, to a perfect man, to the measure of the stature of the fullness of Christ; that we should no longer be children, tossed to and fro and carried about with every wind of doctrine, by the trickery of men, in the cunning craftiness by which they lie in wait to deceive, but, speaking the truth in love, may grow up in all things into Him who is the head—Christ—from whom the whole body, joined and knit together by what every joint supplies, according to the effective working by which every part does its share, causes growth of the body for the edifying of itself in love. (Eph. 4:11–16)

Our ministers must love God, love the Word of God, love to pastor people, have a heart for the lost, and be gifted and trained in their particular areas of ministry. Moreover, they must have a passion for the Vision and Ministry Plan of FPCC and be able to fully support the senior pastor. They are the extensions of the senior pastor and are in their places to carry out his pastoral responsibilities.

Executive Pastor

- Assisting the senior pastor in strategically implementing the Vision and reporting directly to the senior pastor
- Staff leader and mentor to other ministers and directors
- Coordinator of Session and Diaconal Committees
- Coordinator with the church administrator of all church functions as they relate to ordained ministry
- Reporting to this position will be: all ordained ministers
- An administrative assistant will be staffed for the executive pastor.

Minister of Outreach

- Equipping the congregation for personal witnessing (Evangelism Explosion)
- Reaching out to the community through evangelistic seminars, small groups, and other encounters ("3D" or "Alpha")

- Encouraging and coordinating national and international ministries (working with World Missions, Home Missions)
- Liaison for First Friends Ministry to Internationals in the Chattanooga community, and the Reformed University Ministry to University of Tennessee-Chattanooga
- Working with the director of World Missions and the Executive Committee of World Missions to plan, coordinate, and implement the World Missions Conference
- Overseeing the Church-Planting Apprenticeship Program and deploying the church-planting apprentice for meaningful ministry during his term at FPCC
- Overseeing the Outreach and Assimilation Systems Design Plan ("First Touch Ministries")
- Reporting to this position will be: **church-planting apprentice** (who has been assessed by MNA and is in a cooperative program with them)
- This department will share an administrative assistant to ministers.

Minister of Christian Education and Discipleship

- Planning, coordinating, and staffing our volunteers for the Sunday School Ministry from nursery to adults
- Oversight and nurture of all "life groups" of FPCC (Women in the Church, Men of the Covenant, various small groups, Children's Ministry, Youth and Singles Ministry, Senior Adult Ministry)
- Oversight and principle responsibility for leading Wednesday Night Fellowship and Bible Classes
- Oversight of Communicants Classes (children, youth, and adult)

- Responsible for the Summer Institute of the Bible (six Wednesday nights in the summer)
- Responsible for the Spiritual Enrichment Series (annual conference to focus on an aspect of Reformed theology and Life)
- Reporting to this minister will be: **the director of Camp Vesper Point, director (or minister) of youth (with junior high and senior high youth worker interns), director of Children's Ministry, one-year intern for Singles Ministry**
- This department will share an administrative assistant to ministers.

Minister of Congregational Care

- Officer training and development (initial and ongoing)
- Oversight of congregational care groups throughout FPCC
- Responsible for visitation ministries of the church and coordinating those with officers and other ministers
- Leader and trainer for Stephen Ministry
- Leader and trainer for Felt-Need Small Groups (divorce recovery, grief, etc.)
- Reporting to this position will be: **minister of visitation and senior adult ministries**
- This department will share an administrative assistant to ministers.

Director of Music

- Reports directly to the senior pastor
- Adult, children, and youth choirs
- Development of an orchestra and ensemble

- Responsible for all service music in AM and PM services, as well as occasional services of FPCC
- All musical ministries of FPCC
- Coordinating with area musicians to provide occasional and seasonal musical ministry

Church Administrator

- Reports directly to the senior pastor
- Responsible for the day-to-day business management of FPCC
- Staff leader for all nonpastoral staff positions of FPCC

Timetable for Transition

- New senior pastor (Michael A. Milton) is named: December 2001
- Mike Milton begins transition at Kirk O' the Isles PCA, Savannah, GA: December 2001
- Senior pastor moves to the field and assumes ministry: February 2002
- New order of worship services is approved: January 2002
- New weekly worship bulletins are approved and unveiled: February 2002
- Initial Vision and Staffing Plan is unveiled: March 2002
- Appointment of Ad Hoc Committee on Committees and Reorganization: March 2002 (to assess current infrastructure and work with senior pastor to make organizational changes flowing from the Vision for the church)
- Begin search for staff: April 2002
- Senior pastor begins time of visiting similar ministries in the PCA: April 2002

- Senior pastor concentrates on "Listening, Learning, and Loving" as he seeks to build pastoral relationships in the congregation: Ongoing
- Committee on Reorganization approves the Vision Statement and recommends a reorganization of the committee structure to the Session: March 2003
- Session approves the Vision and Ministry Plan; the Ad Hoc Committee on Committees and Reorganization makes its final report: September 2002
- Leadership Retreat for Session and Diaconate: October 25–26, 2002
- Vision and Ministry Plan presented to Congregation: April 2003
- Implementation team formed after congregational meeting: April 2003
- Implementation team presents final report: June 2003
- New organization is in place with the sole purpose of glorifying God, making disciples of Jesus Christ, and realizing the Vision and Mission Plan of FPCC: July 2003

Now to Him who is able to do exceedingly abundantly above all that we ask or think, according to the power that works in us, to Him be glory in the church by Christ Jesus to all generations, forever and ever. Amen. (Eph. 3:20–21)

Notes

Firsthand Testimonials

1. Winston Churchill, *Great Contemporaries: Churchill Reflects on FDR, Hitler, Kipling, Chaplin, Balfour, and Other Giants of His Age*, ed. James W. Muller (Wilmington, DE: ISI Books, 2012), 221.

Chapter One: Let God Come Down!

1. From the transcript of a recording from "Revival in the Hebrides" (1949) by Duncan Campbell, 1968. Accessed online at http://www.christianstogether.net/Articles/94936/Christians_Together _in/Around_the_Region/Western_Isles/Revival_in_the.aspx.

2. D. Martyn Lloyd-Jones, *Revival* (Wheaton, IL: Good News Publishers/Crossway Books, 1987), 198.

Chapter Two: Value the Bible

1. John Calvin, *Commentaries* (Raleigh, NC: Hayes Barton Press, 1958), 74.

2. No one should be surprised, however, that the old battles which were fought, and thought to be won, by evangelicals in the 1970s, are, in fact, back again. Why? Because Satan is not very original. It is for this reason that we should all take time to study church history. Yesterday's heresies too often become today's trends in the church.

3. Cited from an illustration the author heard from John MacArthur at a Ligonier Conference in Orlando, Florida, in 1998.

Chapter Three: Value the Great Commission

1. Quoted in Iain H. Murray, "Robert Murray M'Cheyne," *The Banner of Truth* 4 (December 1955): 14–23, accessed online at http://www.banneroftruth.org/pages/articles/article_print.php?37.

2. "The Ultimate Recall," Paul Lee Tan, ed., *Encyclopedia of 7,700 Illustrations: Signs of the Times* (Rockville, MD: Assurance Publishers, 1979), 543.

3. William Hendriksen, *New Testament Commentary: Exposition of the Gospel According to Luke* (Grand Rapids: Baker Book House, 1978), 755.

4. Samuel Shoemaker, *Extraordinary Living for Ordinary Men* (Grand Rapids: Zondervan, 1966), 139.

5. For information about this poem, written apparently for Shoemaker's congregation on Christmas 1958 at Calvary Rectory, Calvary Episcopal Church, Pittsburgh, Pennsylvania, see http://www.aabibliography.com/dickbhtml/article10.html.

6. Hendriksen, *New Testament Commentary*, 758.

Chapter Four: Value the Heart of the Gospel

1. Mark Water, *The New Encyclopedia of Christian Quotations* (Grand Rapids: Baker Book House, 2000), 442.

2. F. F. Bruce, *Paul: Apostle of the Heart Set Free* (Grand Rapids: Eerdmans, 1977).

3. Robert L. Reymond, *A New Systematic Theology of the Christian Faith* (Nashville: T. Nelson, 1998), xix.

4. For other stories of God's grace in the life of this extraordinary servant of God, see C. John Miller, *A Faith Worth Sharing: A Lifetime of Conversations About Christ* (Phillipsburg, NJ: P&R, 1999).

5. Augustus Toplady, "Rock of Ages" (1776).

6. *Time*, January 12, 1953, "Still Defiant" (see http://www.time .com/time/magazine/article/0,9171,817678,00.html#ixzz1Sa9OdSjf, accessed July 19, 2011).

Chapter Five: Seeing Souls Safe in the Arms of Jesus

1. Matthew Henry, *Matthew Henry's Commentary on the Whole Bible*, new modern ed., 6 vols. (Peabody, MA: Hendrickson Publishers, 1991), on 1 Thess. 2:17–20 (see this citation at: http://bible .wiktel.com/mhc/1_thessalonians/2.html, accessed July 20, 2011).

2. C. S. Lewis, *Mere Christianity*, rev. and enl. ed. (New York: Macmillan, 1955), 118.

Chapter Six: Seeing Christ Triumphant in Our Generation

1. Quoted in Iain H. Murray, *David Martyn Lloyd-Jones: The First Forty Years, 1899–1939* (Carlisle, PA: Banner of Truth Trust, 1982), 226–27.

2. Marcus Dods, *The Gospel of St. John*, 2 vols., Expositor's Bible (London: A. C. Armstrong, 1902), 1:162.

3. Archibald Thomas Robertson, "Word Pictures in the New Testament," Accordance Bible Software, Version 7.1 (2007). See also A. T. Robertson and James A. Swanson, *Word Pictures in the New Testament*, concise ed. (Nashville: Broadman & Holman Publishers, 2000).

4. See John Calvin, *Institutes of the Christian Religion*, ed. John T. McNeill, trans. Ford Lewis Battles, 2 vols. (Louisville: Westminster John Knox Press, 2006).

5. Robertson, "Word Pictures in the New Testament," on John 4:34.

6. Quoted in Murray, *David Martyn Lloyd-Jones: The First Forty Years*, 226–27.

Chapter Seven: Transforming Vision

1. J. C. Ryle, "Eternity!" at http://www.biblebb.com/files/ryle/PR21.htm.

2. Helen Keller, "Optimism" (1903), at http://www.afb.org.

3. Back-cover promotion of Julie K. Norem, *The Positive Power of Negative Thinking: Using Defensive Pessimism to Harness Anxiety and Perform at Your Peak* (New York: Basic Books, 2002).

4. From a personal experience by the author. The name has been changed.

Chapter Eight: Gathering

1. W. T. Stead and G. C. Morgan, *The Welsh Revival* (Boston: The Pilgrim Press, 1905), 13.

2. John Piper, *Let the Nations Be Glad!: The Supremacy of God in Missions* (Grand Rapids: Baker Books, 1993), quoted at http://disciplethenations.org/index10.html, accessed July 20, 2011.

3. Isaac Watts, "When I Survey the Wondrous Cross" (1709). See *The Trinity Hymnal* (Philadelphia: Great Commission Publications, 1990).

Chapter Nine: Growing

1. Mark Water, *The New Encyclopedia of Christian Quotations* (Grand Rapids: Baker Books, 2000), 456.

2. Martin Luther, *Luther's Large Catechism: God's Call to Repentance, Faith, and Prayer, the Bible Plan of Salvation Explained*, trans. J. N. Lenker (Minneapolis: The Luther Press, 1908), 39.

3. Ajith Fernando, *The NIV Application Commentary: Acts* (Grand Rapids: Zondervan, 1998), 119.

4. Eugene H. Peterson. *A Long Obedience in the Same Direction: Discipleship in an Instant Society* (Downers Grove, IL: InterVarsity Press, 1980).

5. Martin Luther, *What Luther Says: An Anthology*, comp. Ewald M. Plass, 3 vols. (St. Louis: Concordia Publishing House, 1959), 2:927. See also the newer one-volume edition of this classic work: *What Luther Says: A Practical In-Home Anthology for the Active Christian*, comp. Ewald M. Plass (St. Louis: Concordia Publishing House, 1986).

6. Ole Hallesby, *Prayer* (Minneapolis: Augsburg, 1994), 204.

7. Ibid.

8. John Piper, *The Legacy of Sovereign Joy: God's Triumphant Grace in the Lives of Augustine, Luther, and Calvin* (Wheaton, IL: Crossway Books, 2000).

Chapter Ten: Sending

1. Charles Haddon Spurgeon, *The Sword and the Trowel, vol. 4, 1874–1876* (Pasadena, TX: Pilgrim Publications, 1978), 102.

2. I have replaced his actual name with this one.

3. "Little children, let us not love in word or talk but in deed and in truth" (1 John 3:18 ESV).

4. "Now those who were scattered went about preaching the word" (Acts 8:4 ESV).

5. Dietrich Bonhoeffer and Robert Coles, *Dietrich Bonhoeffer* (Maryknoll, NY: Orbis Books, 1998), 43.

6. Mark A. Noll, *The Scandal of the Evangelical Mind* (Grand Rapids: Eerdmans, 1995).

7. ἐκκλησία. Key Dictionary of the Greek New Testament: Based upon Strong's Greek Dictionary, Updated for the Critical Greek Text (Accordance Bible Software, 7.1).

8. קָהָל. Key Dictionary of Biblical Hebrew and Aramaic: Based upon Strong's Hebrew Dictionary (Accordance Bible Software, 7.1).

9. עֲצֶרֶת. Key Dictionary of Biblical Hebrew and Aramaic.

10. עֵדָה. Key Dictionary of Biblical Hebrew and Aramaic.

11. Both a theology of the church and a *praxis* of the church are vital to our understanding. I recommend the following books for an initial study of the doctrine and practice of the church: Dietrich Bonhoeffer and John W. Doberstein, *Life Together* (San Francisco: HarperSanFrancisco, 1993); Edmund P. Clowney, *The Church* (Downers Grove, IL: InterVarsity Press, 1995); Mark Dever, *Nine Marks of a Healthy Church*, 4th ed. (Washington: IX Marks Ministries, 2005); Kevin DeYoung and Ted Kluck, *Why We Love the Church: In Praise of Institutions and Organized Religion* (Chicago: Moody Publishers, 2009); Lesslie Newbigin, *The Household of God: Lectures on the Nature of the Church* (New York: Friendship Press, 1954); Lesslie Newbigin, *The Open Secret: Sketches for a Missionary Theology* (Grand Rapids: Eerdmans, 1978); Lesslie Newbigin, *The Gospel in a Pluralist Society* (Grand Rapids: Eerdmans, 1989).

12. Charles Wesley, "And Can It Be That I Should Gain" (1738).

Chapter Eleven: Expository Preaching

1. Quoted in Mark Dever, et. al., *Preaching the Cross* (Wheaton, IL: Crossway, 2007), 66.

2. John R. W. Stott, *Between Two Worlds: The Art of Preaching in the Twentieth Century* (Grand Rapids: Eerdmans, 1982), 15.

3. Bryan Chapell, *Christ-Centered Preaching: Redeeming the Expository Sermon* (Grand Rapids: Baker Books, 1994), 17.

4. Private notes from the General Assembly of the PCA, Los Angeles, California, 1989.

5. For a "novel" (as in the genre of a book, not in theology!) approach to preaching out of the abundance of what God is doing in one's life, I point preachers and parishioners alike to Bruce Mawhinney, *Preaching with Freshness* (Grand Rapids: Kregel Publications, 1997).

6. Presbyterian Church in America, *The Westminster Confession of Faith and Catechisms: As Adopted by the Presbyterian Church in America: With Proof Texts* (Lawrenceville, GA: Christian Education & Publications Committee of the Presbyterian Church in America, 2007).

7. Bryan Chapell, *Christ-Centered Preaching: Redeeming the Expository Sermon*, 2nd ed. (Grand Rapids: Baker Academic, 2005).

8. "And I, when I am lifted up from the earth, will draw all people to myself" (John 12:32 ESV).

9. From personal reflections of conversations with David Nicholas, formerly senior minister of Spanish River Presbyterian Church.

10. For an excellent study of the biblical necessity of announcing the sinfulness of mankind in our preaching and witnessing, see R.C. Sproul, *Saved from What?* (Wheaton, IL: Crossway Books, 2002).

11. Richard Baxter, *Love Breathing Thanks and Praise* (1681), pt. 2, st. 29. This quotation has appeared in numerous books on preaching through the years, without citation, since it has become a veritable "prayer of illumination" for the Protestant church before preaching. See, for example, David Martyn Lloyd-Jones, *Preaching and Preachers* (Grand Rapids: Zondervan Publishing House, 1972), 86.

12. Eric Alexander, *What Is Biblical Preaching?* (Phillipsburg, NJ: P&R Publishing, 2008), 11.

Chapter Twelve: Living Worship

1. *Give Praise to God: A Vision for Reforming Worship; Celebrating the Legacy of James Montgomery Boice*, ed. Philip Graham Ryken (Phillipsburg, NJ: P&R, 2003), 435.

2. Jeremiah Burroughs, *Gospel Worship: Or the Right Manner of Sanctifying the Name of God in General, and Particularly in These 3 Great Ordinances, 1. Hearing the Word, 2. Receiving the Lord's Supper, 3. Prayer* (Ligonier, PA: Soli Deo Gloria Publications, 1990).

3. A. W. Tozer and Gerald B. Smith, *Whatever Happened to Worship?* (Camp Hill, PA: Christian Publications, 1985), 7.

4. John R. W. Stott and Timothy Dudley-Smith, *Authentic Christianity* (Downers Grove, IL: InterVarsity Press, 1995), 73.

5. T. David Gordon, *Why Johnny Can't Sing Hymns: How Pop Culture Rewrote the Hymnal* (Phillipsburg, NJ: P&R Publications, 2010).

6. Terry Johnson, *Leading in Worship: A Sourcebook for Presbyterian Students and Ministers Drawing upon the Biblical and Historic Forms of the Reformed Tradition* (Oak Ridge, TN: Covenant Foundation, 1996), 2.

7. See R. J. Gore, *Covenantal Worship: Reconsidering the Puritan Regulative Principle* (Phillipsburg, NJ: P&R Publications, 2002).

8. G. Campbell Morgan, *The Gospel According to John* (New York: Fleming H. Revell Co., 1933), 76.

9. Bryan Chapell, *Christ-Centered Worship: Letting the Gospel Shape Our Practice* (Grand Rapids: Baker Academic, 2009), 134.

10. From personal experience of worship at National Presbyterian Church when Dr. Barnes was the pastor there.

11. Evelyn Underhill, *Worship* (New York: Crossroad, 1982), 62.

12. Ibid., 9.

Chapter Thirteen: Loving Fellowship

1. Mark Water, *The New Encyclopedia of Christian Quotations* (Grand Rapids: Baker Books, 2000), 368.

2. See, for example, Brian Habig and Les Newsom, *The Enduring Community: Embracing the Priority of the Church* (Jackson, MS: Reformed University Press, 2001).

3. For a fuller treatment of hospitality in the church according to the Scriptures, see Alexander Strauch, *The Hospitality Commands: Building Loving Christian Community: Building Bridges and Neighbors* (Littleton, CO: Lewis and Roth Publishers, 1993).

4. Tremper Longman, David E. Garland, et. al., *The Expositor's Bible Commentary, vol. 10: Luke–Acts*, rev. ed. (Grand Rapids: Zondervan, 2007), 568.

5. R. L. Stevenson, *Lay Morals: And Other Papers* (New York: C. Scribner's Sons, 1915), 50.

6. Paul Lee Tan, *Encyclopedia of 7700 Illustrations* (Rockville, MD: Assurance Publishers, 1979), 568.

Chapter Fourteen: Compassionate Outreach

1. Mark Water, *The New Encyclopedia of Christian Quotations* (Grand Rapids: Baker Books, 2000), 672.

2. Bob Logan and Larry Short, *Mobilizing for Compassion: Moving People into Ministry* (Grand Rapids: Fleming H. Revell, 1994).

3. See Arnold A. Dallimore, *Spurgeon* (Chicago: Moody Press, 1984); Lewis A. Drummond, *Spurgeon: Prince of Preachers* (Grand Rapids: Kregel Publications, 1992).

4. Charles Colson, "Will the Church Miss the Volunteer Revolution?" *Christianity Today*, 36.3 (1992): 88.

5. From my personal illustration files.

6. For a good, practical example of this ministry, see Timothy J. Keller and Presbyterian Church in America, *Resources for Deacons: Love Expressed Through Mercy Ministries* (Lawrenceville, GA: Christian Education and Publications [of the Presbyterian Church in America], 1985).

Chapter Fifteen: It's All We Have, But It's All We Need

1. Mark Water, *The New Encyclopedia of Christian Quotations* (Grand Rapids: Baker Books, 2000), 783.

2. "Finally, be strong in the Lord and in the strength of his might. Put on the whole armor of God, that you may be able to stand against the schemes of the devil. For we do not wrestle against

flesh and blood, but against the rulers, against the authorities, against the cosmic powers over this present darkness, against the spiritual forces of evil in the heavenly places" (Eph. 6:10–12 ESV).

3. John Piper, *Let the Nations Be Glad!: The Supremacy of God in Missions*, 2nd ed. (Grand Rapids: Baker Academic, 2003), 69.

4. Martin Luther, *Selections from the Table Talk of Martin Luther*, trans. Henry Bell (repr., Kessinger Publishing, 2004), 69.

5. Michael Bronson, *The Incredible Power of Prayer* (BibleHelp .org, 2003), 24.

6. Thomas Benson Pollock, "The Church's One Foundation" (1871).

Resources for Further Study

Alexander, Eric. *What Is Biblical Preaching?* Basics of the Reformed Faith. Phillipsburg, NJ: P&R Publishing, 2008.

Bonhoeffer, Dietrich, and John W. Doberstein. *Life Together.* San Francisco: HarperSanFrancisco, 1993.

Bonhoeffer, Dietrich, and Robert Coles. *Dietrich Bonhoeffer.* Modern Spiritual Masters Series. Maryknoll, NY: Orbis Books, 1998.

Bruce, F. F. *Paul, Apostle of the Heart Set Free.* Grand Rapids: Eerdmans, 1977.

Burroughs, Jeremiah. *Gospel Worship: Or the Right Manner of Sanctifying the Name of God in General, and Particularly in These 3 Great Ordinances, 1. Hearing the Word, 2. Receiving the Lord's Supper, 3. Prayer.* Ligonier, PA: Soli Deo Gloria Publications, 1990.

Calvin, John. *Institutes of the Christian Religion.* Edited by John T. McNeill. Translated by John T. McNeill. 2 vols. The Library of Christian Classics. Louisville: Westminster John Knox Press, 2006.

Chapell, Bryan. *Christ-Centered Preaching: Redeeming the Expository Sermon.* Grand Rapids: Baker Books, 1994. (Second edition, Baker Academic, 2005.)

——————. *Christ-Centered Worship: Letting the Gospel Shape Our Practice.* Grand Rapids: Baker Academic, 2009.

Clowney, Edmund P. *The Church.* Contours of Christian Theology. Downers Grove, IL: InterVarsity Press, 1995.

Dallimore, Arnold A. *Spurgeon.* Chicago: Moody Press, 1984.

Dever, Mark. *Nine Marks of a Healthy Church.* 4th edition. Washington: IX Marks Ministries, 2005.

DeYoung, Kevin, and Ted Kluck. *Why We Love the Church: In Praise of Institutions and Organized Religion.* Chicago: Moody Publishers, 2009.

Dods, Marcus. *The Gospel of St. John.* 2 vols. Expositor's Bible. London: Hodder and Stoughton, 1896.

Drummond, Lewis A. *Spurgeon: Prince of Preachers.* Grand Rapids: Kregel Publications, 1992.

Gordon, T. David. *Why Johnny Can't Sing Hymns: How Pop Culture Rewrote the Hymnal.* Phillipsburg, NJ: P&R Publications, 2010.

Gore, R. J. *Covenantal Worship: Reconsidering the Puritan Regulative Principle.* Phillipsburg, NJ: P&R Publications, 2002.

Habig, Brian, and Les Newsom. *The Enduring Community: Embracing the Priority of the Church.* Jackson, MS: Reformed University Press, 2001.

Hallesby, Ole. *Prayer.* Minneapolis: Augsburg, 1994.

Hendriksen, William. *New Testament Commentary: Exposition of the Gospel According to Luke.* Grand Rapids: Baker Book House, 1978.

Henry, Matthew. *Matthew Henry's Commentary on the Whole Bible.* New modern ed. 6 vols. Peabody, MA: Hendrickson Publishers, 1991.

Johnson, Terry. *Leading in Worship: A Sourcebook for Presbyterian Students and Ministers Drawing upon the Biblical and Historic Forms of the Reformed Tradition.* Oak Ridge, TN: Covenant Foundation, 1996.

Keller, Timothy J., and Presbyterian Church in America. *Resources for Deacons: Love Expressed Through Mercy Ministries.* [Lawrenceville, GA]: Christian Education and Publications [of the Presbyterian Church in America], 1985.

Lewis, C. S. *Mere Christianity.* Rev. and enl. ed. New York: Macmillan, 1955.

Lloyd-Jones, David Martyn. *Preaching and Preachers.* Grand Rapids: Zondervan Publishing House, 1972.

Logan, Bob, and Larry Short. *Mobilizing for Compassion: Moving People into Ministry.* Grand Rapids: Fleming H. Revell, 1994.

Longman, Tremper, David E. Garland, and others. *Luke–Acts*. Expositor's Bible Commentary, rev. ed. Grand Rapids: Zondervan, 2007.

Luther, Martin. *The Large Catechism of Martin Luther*. Reprint, Forgotten Books, 2007.

——————. *Selections from the Table Talk of Martin Luther*. Translated by Henry Bell. Kessinger Publishing, 2004.

——————. *What Luther Says, an Anthology*. Compiled by Ewald M. Plass. 3 vols. St. Louis: Concordia Publishing House, 1959.

——————. *What Luther Says: A Practical In-Home Anthology for the Active Christian*. Compiled by Ewald M. Plass. St. Louis: Concordia Publishing House, 1986.

Mawhinney, Bruce. *Preaching with Freshness*. Grand Rapids: Kregel Publications, 1997.

Menninger, Karl A. *Whatever Became of Sin?* New York: Hawthorn Books, 1973.

Miller, C. John. *A Faith Worth Sharing: A Lifetime of Conversations About Christ*. Phillipsburg, NJ: P&R, 1999.

Morgan, G. Campbell. *The Gospel According to John*. New York: Fleming H. Revell Co., 1933.

Newbigin, Lesslie. *The Gospel in a Pluralist Society*. Grand Rapids: Eerdmans, 1989.

——————. *The Household of God: Lectures on the Nature of the Church*. New York: Friendship Press, 1954.

——————. *The Open Secret: Sketches for a Missionary Theology*. Grand Rapids: Eerdmans, 1978.

Noll, Mark A. *The Scandal of the Evangelical Mind*. Grand Rapids: Eerdmans, 1995.

Piper, John. *Let the Nations Be Glad! The Supremacy of God in Missions*. Grand Rapids: Baker Books, 1993.

——————. *The Legacy of Sovereign Joy: God's Triumphant Grace in the Lives of Augustine, Luther, and Calvin*. Wheaton, IL: Crossway Books, 2000.

Presbyterian Church in America. *The Westminster Confession of Faith and Catechisms: As Adopted by the Presbyterian Church in*

America: With Proof Texts. Lawrenceville, GA: Christian Education & Publications Committee of the Presbyterian Church in America, 2007.

Reymond, Robert L. *A New Systematic Theology of the Christian Faith*. Nashville: T. Nelson, 1998.

Robertson, A. T., and James A. Swanson. *Word Pictures in the New Testament*. Concise edition. Nashville: Broadman & Holman Publishers, 2000.

Shoemaker, Samuel M. *Revive Thy Church Beginning with Me*. Waco, TX: Word Books, 1948.

Sproul, R.C. *Saved from What?* Wheaton, IL: Crossway Books, 2002.

Stott, John R. W., and Timothy Dudley-Smith. *Authentic Christianity*. Downers Grove, IL: InterVarsity Press, 1995.

Stott, John R. W. *Between Two Worlds: The Art of Preaching in the Twentieth Century*. Grand Rapids: Eerdmans, 1982.

Strauch, Alexander. *The Hospitality Commands: Building Loving Christian Community: Building Bridges and Neighbors*. Littleton, CO: Lewis and Roth Publishers, 1993.

The Trinity Hymnal. Philadelphia: Great Commission Publications, 1990.

Tozer, A. W., and Gerald B. Smith. *Whatever Happened to Worship?* Camp Hill, PA: Christian Publications, 1985.

Underhill, Evelyn. *Worship*. New York: Crossroad, 1982.

Waters, Mark. *The New Encyclopedia of Christian Quotations*. Grand Rapids: Baker Books, 2000.

Also by MICHAEL A. MILTON

Sicknesses, spiritual depression, disabilities, painful memories, strained relationships . . . all of these weigh on our hearts at one time or another. Yet even in the midst of our heartache, a faith comes from Jesus Christ that not only encourages us through our pain, but also *transforms* our pain . . . as long as we let it.

These pastoral messages and personal illustrations show how brokenhearted Christians can locate the God of all comfort in the center of their pain. Learn how the gospel transforms our private pain into personal praise and turns our weakest, most discouraging moments into our best, most uplifting moments.

"Mike's book won me immediately. You can tell that Mike has been a pastor and someone who has suffered personally. Pastors and sufferers can never be content with a theoretical answer to suffering. You must wisely develop a practical theology of suffering. *Songs in the Night* is just that."
  —**Tim Lane, President,** The Christian Counseling and
    Educational Foundation

Also by MICHAEL A. MILTON

"Where did you find God today?"

This question from a pastor to his congregation is at the heart of these inspiring stories. Mike Milton takes you on a journey through experiences, events, relationships, and private recollections—all pursuing the goal of finding God's grace at work in everyday life.

Join him as these seemingly "small things" bring a tear, a smile, and a renewed appreciation for God's presence in your own life, as long as you are willing to look.

"A pleasure to read. Warm, encouraging, inspiring, and uplifting."
—**Sally Lloyd-Jones,** Author of *The Jesus Storybook Bible*

"Mike Milton has been finding God in the ordinary from his first childhood day of poverty in Louisiana, in everything from cinnamon rolls to Old Spice, from hollyhocks to hurricanes. With a pastor's heart, he obviously longs for us to find him as well."
—**Michael Card,** Singer-Songwriter and Author

More Church Resources from P&R

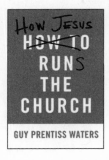

Few books on church leadership explore the biblical foundations of church government. This one does—providing pastors, elders, students, and laypeople with a greater understanding of what the church is and how it should be governed.

Waters also examines the offices that Jesus has appointed in the church and investigates how elders in particular are to serve her.

"Ecclesiology has for too long been the poor relation in evangelical and even Reformed circles. Recent years have witnessed a welcome reaction against such neglect, but much of this has not been well grounded either biblically or historically. Thus, it is a pleasure to commend Guy Waters's book as a sound, biblical, accessible guide to the nature of the church. Written by a churchman for the church, it can be read with profit by office-bearers, Sunday school teachers, and any believer who wants a deeper grasp of what it means to be a member of Christ's church on earth."

—**Carl R. Trueman,** Professor of Historical Theology and Church History, Westminster Theological Seminary

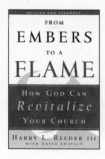

Whether your church is healthy or struggling, the biblical principles in this book point the way to greater spiritual vitality. A pastor, seminary teacher, and conference speaker, Harry Reeder has long specialized in church revitalization. Reeder and Swavely deftly alert us to potential problems in our churches, help us recognize our weaknesses and opportunities, and guide us in applying biblically based strategies for rekindling the flames of godly growth.

"Harry Reeder is more than a great preacher—he is gifted at spiritually revitalizing local congregations. And unless your church is a brand-new church plant, it needs some level of renewal! So we all can learn much from this volume."
—**Timothy J. Keller,** Senior Pastor, Redeemer Presbyterian Church, Manhattan

"I highly recommend this book. Harry Reeder is well qualified to write on church revitalization. He has seen two churches dramatically revitalized under his leadership and has for years coached other churches in the principles through seminars and ongoing consultation. This is an extremely important area, and Harry is an expert in the field."
—**Frank M. Barker Jr.,** Pastor Emeritus, Briarwood Presbyterian Church, Birmingham, Alabama

More Church Leadership Resources from P&R

To rediscover God's gift of eldership for the church today, we need to go back beyond the New Testament to the origins of the office of elder in ancient Israel. There we discover the enduring principles that guided the elder in antiquity—and that guide the church today. In this book you will develop a renewed understanding of the office of elder and of godly discipline.

The Explorations in Biblical Theology series addresses the need for quality literature that attracts believing readers to good theology and builds them up in their faith. Each title in the series combines satisfying content with the accessibility and readability of a popular book. The result is a valuable addition to the library of any college senior, seminarian, pastor—indeed, anyone concerned to know what the Bible really says.

"Cornelis Van Dam provides a full and intelligent discussion of the biblical texts that inform our understanding of the office of the elder in the church today. This book is a must for those who are elders or who think they might be called to that office."
　　—Tremper Longman III, Westminster Theological Seminary, Philadelphia

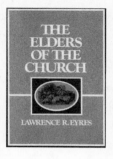

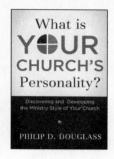

In this thorough, practical study of biblical church government, Eyers discusses the ruling elder, the teaching elder, the biblical principles of each, and more.

"Mr. Eyers's study grows out of a mature exposure to the problems of biblical church government. He is at once theoretical and practical. By exegetical work, he not only endeavors to uncover biblical principles, but from them also draws implications and makes applications in useful workaday terms."

—**Jay E. Adams,** Dean, Institute for Nouthetic Studies

"Pours that wealth of experience and scholarship into an immensely helpful book that will help pastors, lay people, and pastoral search committees understand the personality of their churches so they can plan and staff according to their unique mix of gifts rather than according to naive assumptions, idealistic expectations, or simplistic reactions. . . . The observations are keen, the advice is sage, and the practical help will provide new hope to many."

—**Bryan Chapell,** Chancellor, Covenant Theological Seminary, St. Louis, Missouri

More Church Leadership Resources from P&R

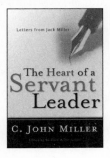

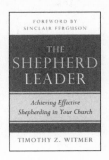

Miller gently challenges those called to serve as leaders to find their primary motivation in the glory of God alone. These pastoral letters serve as models of compassionate leadership, as Miller provides counsel on ministry issues, physical suffering, overcoming sin, learning to forgive, and spiritual warfare.

"Jack Miller's warm and personal letters are an extension of the man himself—a spiritual father to so many. Each letter caused me to search my heart and pointed me to Jesus."
—**Susan Hunt,** Author and Consultant, Christian Education and Publications, Presbyterian Church in America

Leaders in the church are called to be shepherds, not a board of directors. This requires involvement in a personal shepherding ministry among the people. *The Shepherd Leader* unpacks the four primary ministries of shepherds—knowing, feeding, leading, and protecting—on macro (church-wide) and micro (personal) levels, providing seven elements to be incorporated into an effective shepherding plan.

"For leaders who long to be faithful in the field, this book offers a wealth of theological and practical insight that will strengthen your hand."
—**Dave Harvey,** Sovereign Grace Ministries, Author of *When Sinners Say "I Do"*

Missions Resources from P&R

Like the wounded man on the Jericho road, there are needy people in our path—the widow next door, the family strapped with medical bills, the homeless man outside our place of worship. God calls us to be ministers of mercy to people in need of shelter, assistance, medical care, or just friendship.

Timothy Keller demonstrates that caring for needy people is the job of every believer—not just church deacons—as fundamental to Christian living as evangelism, nurture, and worship. But Keller doesn't stop there. He shows *how* we can carry out this vital ministry as individuals, families, and churches.

Along the way, he deals perceptively with many thorny issues, such as the costs of meeting needs versus the limits of time and resources, giving material aid versus teaching responsibility, and meeting needs within the church versus those outside.

"*Ministries of Mercy* is a solid piece of work, the best of its kind that I have yet seen. It is concrete, down-to-earth, spelling out in specific detail every phase of what Keller calls the ministry of mercy."
   —**Vernon C. Grounds,** Chancellor, Denver Seminary, Littleton, Colorado